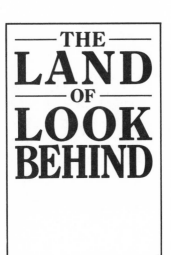

Für Jeannine !
Zum Geburtstage 1991.

Also by Michelle Cliff:

The Winner Names the Age, ed.

Claiming an Identity They Taught Me to Despise

Abeng

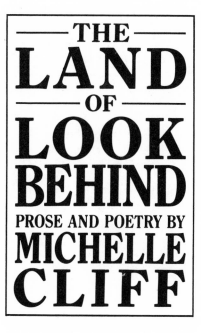

THE
LAND
OF
LOOK
BEHIND

PROSE AND POETRY BY
MICHELLE
CLIFF

Firebrand Books

Ithaca, New York 14850

Parts of this book, some in slightly different form, appeared in *Azalea, Conditions, Feminary, Heresies, Ikon, Iowa Review;* in the collection *Claiming an Identity They Taught Me to Despise* (Persephone Press, 1981); and in the anthology *Home Girls,* ed. Barbara Smith (Kitchen Table: Women of Color Press, 1983).

My thanks are due to Nancy K. Bereano for her intelligence and vision, and to Mary A. Scott for her skill and sensitivity.

Book and cover design by Mary A. Scott
Typesetting by Lois J. Brooke (The Gregory Paul Press, Inc.)

Printed in the United States of America by McNaughton & Gunn, Inc.

Library of Congress Cataloging-in-Publication Data

Cliff, Michelle.
    The land of Look Behind.

    I. Title.
PR9265.9.C55   1985   818   85-16159
ISBN 0-932379-09-5
ISBN 0-932379-08-7 (pbk.)

This book is for Audre Lorde

Contents

Preface   11
    A Journey into Speech

from Claiming an Identity They Taught Me to Despise   19
    Passing / Obsolete Geography / Against Granite /
    A History of Costume / Claiming an Identity They
    Taught Me to Despise / The Garden

Travel Notes   53

If I Could Write This in Fire, I Would Write This in Fire   57

Love in the Third World   77
    The Land of Look Behind / Make It Your Own /
    The Laughing Mulatto (Formerly a Statue) Speaks
    / Within the Veil / Heartache / Jaffrey Center, New
    Hampshire / The Crazy Teepee / Artificial Skin /
    Constructive Engagement / Battle Royal /
    Love in the Third World

A Pilgrimage, a History Lesson, Two Satires, and a
    Vision   104
    A Visit to the Secret Annex / Europe Becomes
    Blacker / A Visit from Mr. Botha /
    I-tie-all-my-people-together

July 31st. I do indeed dread a long passage, for the smell of the sugar is so bad, it destroys everything. All the cabin is covered with a sort of leaden surface, which comes off upon one's clothes, and even our skins seem to be dyed with it. . . .I constantly feel my throat and lungs affected by it. Everything *tastes* of the *smell* of the sugar, and I am in continual apprehension. . . .

Lady Maria Nugent, on her return to England
from Jamaica, 1805

There is no sense in hate; it comes back to you. Therefore, make your history so laudable, magnificent, and untarnished, that another generation will not seek to repay [you]. . . . The bones of injustice have a peculiar way of rising from the tombs to plague and mock the iniquitous.

Marcus Garvey

Preface

A Journey into Speech

The first piece of writing I produced, beyond a dissertation on intellectual game-playing in the Italian Renaissance, was entitled "Notes on Speechlessness," published in *Sinister Wisdom,* no. 5. In it I talked about my identification with Victor, the wild boy of Aveyron, who, after his rescue from the forest and wildness by a well-meaning doctor of Enlightenment Europe, became "civilized," but never came to speech. I felt, with Victor, that my wildness had been tamed—that which I had been taught was my wildness.

My dissertation was produced at the Warburg Institute, University of London, and was responsible for giving me an intellectual belief in myself that I had not had before, while at the same time distancing me from who I am, almost rendering me speechless about who I am. At least I believed in the young woman who wrote the dissertation—still, I wondered who she was and where she had come from.

11

I could speak fluently, but I could not reveal. I immersed myself in the social circles and academies of Siena, Florence, Urbino, as well as Venice, creating a place for myself there, and describing this ideal world in eloquent linear prose.

When I began, finally, partly through participation in the feminist movement, to approach myself as a subject, my writing was jagged, nonlinear, almost shorthand. The "Notes on Speechlessness" were indeed notes, written in snatches on a nine-to-five job. I did not choose the noteform consciously; a combination of things drew me to it. An urgency for one thing. I also felt incompetent to construct an essay in which I would describe the intimacies, fears, and lies I wrote of in "Speechlessness." I felt my thoughts, things I had held within for a lifetime, traversed so wide a terrain, had so many stops and starts, apparent nonsequiturs, that an essay—with its cold-blooded dependence on logical construction, which I had mastered practically against my will—could not work. My subject could not respond to that form, which would have contradicted the idea of speechlessness. This tender approach to myself within the confines and interruptions of a forty-hour-a-week job and against a history of forced fluency was the beginning of a journey into speech.

To describe this journey further, I must begin at the very beginning, with origins, and the significance of these origins. How they have made me the writer I am.

I originate in the Caribbean, specifically on the island of Jamaica, and although I have lived in the United States and in England, I travel as a Jamaican. It is Jamaica that forms my writing for the most part, and which has formed for the most part, myself. Even though I often feel what Derek Walcott expresses in his poem "The Schooner *Flight*": "I had no nation now but the imagination." It is a complicated business.

Jamaica is a place halfway between Africa and England, to put it simply, although historically one culture (guess which one) has been esteemed and the other denigrated (both are understatements)—at least among those who control the culture and politics of the island—the Afro-Saxons. As a child among these people, indeed of these people, as one of them, I received the message of anglocentrism, of white supremacy, and I internalized it. As a writer, as a human being, I have had to accept that reality and deal with its effect on me, as well as finding what has been lost to me from the darker side, and what may be hidden, to be dredged from memory and dream. And it *is* there to be dredged. As my writing delved longer and deeper into this part of myself, I began to dream and imagine. I was able to clearly envision Nanny, the leader of a group of guerrilla fighters known as the Windward Maroons, as she is described: an old Black woman naked except for a necklace made from the teeth of whitemen. I began to love her.

It is a long way from the court of Urbino to Nanny the Coromantyn warrior.

One of the effects of assimilation, indoctrination, passing into the anglocentrism of British West Indian culture is that you believe absolutely in the hegemony of the King's English and in the form in which it is meant to be expressed. Or else your writing is not literature; it is folklore, and folklore can never be art. Read some poetry by West Indian writers—some, not all—and you will see what I mean. You have to dissect stanza after extraordinarily anglican stanza for Afro-Caribbean truth; you may never find the latter. But this has been our education. The anglican ideal—Milton, Wordsworth, Keats—was held before us with an assurance that we were unable, and would never be enabled, to compose a work of similar correctness. No reggae spoken here.

Coromantyn, or Coromantee, was used by the British in Jamaica to describe slaves from the Gold Coast of Africa, especially slaves who spoke Akan.

To write as a complete Caribbean woman, or man for that matter, demands of us retracing the African part of ourselves, reclaiming as our own, and as our subject, a history sunk under the sea, or scattered as potash in the canefields, or gone to bush, or trapped in a class system notable for its rigidity and absolute dependence on color stratification. On a past bleached from our minds. It means finding the artforms of these of our ancestors and speaking in the *patois* forbidden us. It means realizing our knowledge will always be wanting. It means also, I think, mixing in the forms taught us by the oppressor, undermining his language and co-opting his style, and turning it to our purpose. In my current work-in-progress, a novel, I alternate the King's English with *patois,* not only to show the class background of characters, but to show how Jamaicans operate within a split consciousness. It would be as dishonest to write the novel entirely in *patois* as to write entirely in the King's English. Neither is the novel a linear construction; its subject is the political upheavals of the past twenty years. Therefore, I have mixed time and incident and space and character and also form to try to mirror the historical turbulence.

For another example, included in this volume is a long poem, actually half-poem, half-prose, in which I imagine the visit of Botha of South Africa to the heads of western Europe in the summer of 1984. I wrote this as a parody of Gilbert and Sullivan because their work epitomizes salient aspects of the British Empire which remain vibrant. And because as a child I was sick to death of hearing "I am the very model of a modern major general." I enjoyed writing this, playing with rhyme and language—it was like spitting into their cultural soup.

We are a fragmented people. My experience as a writer coming from a culture of colonialism, a culture of Black people riven from each other, my struggle to get wholeness from fragmentation while working within fragmentation, producing work which may find its strength in its depiction of fragmentation, through form as well as content, is similar to the experience of other writers whose origins are in countries defined by colonialism.

Ama Ata Aidoo, the Ghanaian writer, in her extraordinary book, *Our Sister Killjoy or Reflections from a Black-Eyed Squint*, plots this fragmentation, and shows how both the demand and solace of the so-called mother country can claim us, while we long for our homeland and are shamed for it and ourselves at the same time. The form Aidoo uses to depict this dilemma of colonial peoples—part prose, fictional and epistolary, part poetry—illustrates the fragmentation of the heroine and grasps the fury of the heroine, living in Europe but drawn back to Ghana, knowing she can never be European. She will only be a been-to; that is, one who has been to the mother country. *Our Sister Killjoy* affected me directly, not just because like Aidoo's heroine I was a been-to. I was especially drawn by the way in which Aidoo expresses rage against colonialism—crystallized for her by the whiteman she calls the "Christian Doctor" throughout, excising Black African hearts to salvage white South African lives. In her expression of the rage she feels her prose breaks apart sharply into a staccato poetry—direct, short, brilliantly bitter—as if measured prose would disintegrate under her fury.

I wanted that kind of directness in my writing, as I came into closer contact with my rage, and a realization that rage could fuel and shape my work. As a light-skinned colonial girlchild, both in Jamaica and in the Jamaican milieu of my family abroad, rage was the last thing expected of me.

After reading Aidoo I knew I wanted to tell exactly how things were, what had been done, to us and by us, without muddying the issue with conventional beauty, avoiding be-

NOK Publishers, Lagos and New York, 1979.

coming trapped in the grace of language for its own sake, which is always seductive.

In *Claiming an Identity They Taught Me to Despise*, a piece published before I read Aidoo, halfway between poetry and prose, as I am halfway between Africa and England, patriot and expatriate, white and Black, I felt my use of language and imagery had sometimes masked what I wanted to convey. It seemed sometimes that the reader was able to ignore what I was saying while admiring the way in which it was said.

And yet, *Claiming* is an honest self-portrait of who I was at the time. Someone who was unable, for the most part, to recapture the native language of Jamaica, and who relied on the King's English and European allusions, but who wrote from a feminist consciousness and a rapidly evolving consciousness of colonialism, and a knowlege of self-hatred. Someone who also dreamed in Latin—as I did and as I recorded in the title section, included here. *Claiming*'s strengths, I think, are in the more intimate, private places of the piece, which I constructed much as the "Notes on Speechlessness" are constructed. Shorthand—almost—as memory and dream emerge; fast, at once keen, at once incomplete. I was also, in those sections, laboring under the ancient taboos of the assimilated: don't tell outsiders anything real about yourself. Don't reveal *our* secrets to *them*. Don't make us seem foolish, or oppressed. Write it quickly before someone catches you. Before you catch yourself.

After reading *Our Sister Killjoy*, something was set loose in me, I directed rage outward rather than inward, and I was able to write a piece called "If I Could Write This in Fire I Would Write This in Fire." In it I let myself go, any thought of approval for my words vanished; I strung together myth, dream, historical detail, observation, as I had done before, but I added native language, tore into the indoctrination of the colonizer, surprised myself with the violence of my words.

That piece of writing led to other pieces, collected in this volume, in which I try to depict personal fragmentation and describe political reality, according to the peculiar lens of the colonized.

Santa Cruz, CA
May 1985

from Claiming an Identity They Taught Me to Despise

Passing

I

> The mystery of the world is the visible, not the invisible.
>
> Oscar Wilde

Camouflage: ground lizards in the schoolyard rustle under a pile of leaves—some are deep-green, others shiny blue: all blend in. I fear they might be there—even when there is no sound.

To this day camouflage terrorizes me.

The pattern of skin which makes a being invisible against its habitat.

And—yes—this camouflage exists for its protection. I am not what I seem to be.

I must make myself visible against my habitat. But there exists a certain danger in peeling back. The diamondback without her mottled skin loses a level of defense.

The onlooker may be startled to recognize the visible being. The onlooker may react with disbelief: sometimes, with recognition.

II

I am remembering: women in Jamaica asking to touch my hair.

On a map from 1740 which hangs above my desk I can see the place where my grandmother now lives. Old-womans Savannah. That is the place which holds colors for me. The other seems a shadow-life.

I am remembering: in the hard dirt in the bright sun between the house and the shed which is a kitchen my mother sat— after church—on a wooden crate. Under the box a headless chicken flapped its wings.

Quiet. Then she rose—removed the box. Plunged the carcass into boiling water to loosen the feathers.

She passed the carcass to her mother who cut and stewed Sunday dinner.

I watched this all in wonder. The two women were almost silent.

III

I thought it was only the loss of the mother—
but it was also the loss of others:
who grew up to work for us
and stood at the doorway while the t.v. played
and stood at the doorway while we told ghost-stories
and ironed the cloths for the tea-trays.
but this division existed even then—

Passing demands a desire to become invisible. A ghost-life. An ignorance of connections.

IV

In America: each year the day before school after summer vacation I sat on my bed touching my notebooks, pencils, ruler—holding the stern and sweet-smelling brown oxfords in my lap and spreading my skirt and blouse and underwear and socks before me. My mother would come in and always say the same thing: "Free paper burn now."

Such words conspire to make a past.
Such words conjure a knowledge.
Such words make assimilation impossible. They stay with you for years. They puzzle, but you sense a significance. I need these words.

V

People call my grandmother the miracle of the loaves and the fishes. People used to fill the yard at dinnertime with their enamel bowls and utensils waiting to be fed. And she managed to feed them all. Whether rice or yam or green banana cooked in dried saltfish.

In America this food became a secret—and a link. Shopping under the bridge with my mother for cho-cho and cassava and breadfruit. And the New Home Bakery for hard-dough bread. Finding a woman who makes paradise plums.

The church we belong to is having a West Indian dinner and my mother has agreed to share her food. The church hall is crowded. But the groups do not mix. One white woman carefully removes a chewed piece of green banana from her mouth and slides it to the side of her plate.

My mother sees this. She says nothing.

Passing demands quiet. And from that quiet—silence.

VI

Something used by someone else carries a history with it. A piece of cloth, a platter, a cut-glass pitcher, a recipe.

A history and a spirit. You want to know when it was used. And how. And what it wants from you.

Passing demands you keep that knowledge to yourself.

VII

In Jamaica we are as common as ticks.
We graft the Bombay onto the common mango. The Valencia onto the Seville. We mix tangerines and oranges. We create mules.

Under British rule—Zora Neale Hurston writes about this—we could have ourselves declared legally white. The rationale was that it made us better servants.

This symbolic skin was carried to the United States where passing was easy.

Isolate yourself. If they find out about you it's all over. Forget about your great-grandfather with the darkest skin—until you're back "home" where they joke about how he climbed a

coconut tree when he was eighty. Go to college. Go to England
to study. Learn about the Italian Renaissance and forget that
they kept slaves. Ignore the tears of the Indians. Black
Americans don't understand us either. We are—after all—
British. If anyone asks you, talk about sugar plantations and
the Maroons—not the landscape of downtown Kingston or the
children at the roadside. Be selective. Cultivate normalcy.
Stress sameness. Blend in. For God's sake don't pile difference
upon difference. It's not safe.

Back on the island the deep-purple skin of the ripe fruit
conceals a center which holds a star-shape. Sitting in the
branches one afternoon with a friend we eat ourselves into an
intimacy in which we talk about our families. He is fourteen and
works for my grandmother. I am twelve. He tells me his
grandmother was East Indian and therefore he is not com-
pletely black. I tell him I am white—showing my sunburnt
nose—explaining only white skin burns. He laughs. Then we
scuffle.

It is like trying to remember a dream in which the images slip
and slide. The words connect and disconnect and you wake
feeling senseless.

"No strange news" my grandmother often closes her letters.

We are not exotic—or aromatic—or poignant.
We are not aberrations. We are ordinary.
All this has happened before.

Obsolete Geography

I

Airplane shadows moved across the mountains, leaving me to clear rivers, dancing birds, sweet fruits. Sitting on a river rock, my legs dangle in the water. I am twelve—and solitary.

II

On a hillside I search for mangoes. As I shake the tree the fruit drops: its sweetness splits at my feet. I suck the remaining flesh from the hairy seed. The sap from the stem stains my lips—to fester later. I am warned I may be scarred.

III

My other life of notebooks, lessons, homework continues. I try not to pay it mind.

IV

Things that live here: star apple, pineapple, custard apple, south sea apple; tamarind, ginep, avocado, guava, cashew, cane; yellow, white, St. Vincent yam; red, black, pepper ants; bats, scorpions, nightingales, spiders; cassava, sweetsop, soursop, cho-cho, okra, guango, mahoe, mahogany, ackee, plaintain, chinese banana; poly lizard, green lizard, croaking lizard, ground lizard.

V

The pig is big, and hangs suspended by her hind legs from a tree in the yard. She is screaming—her agony not self-conscious. I have been told not to watch her slaughter, but my twelve-year-old self longs for the flow of blood. A small knife is inserted in her throat, pulled back and forth until the throat slits, the wound widens, and blood runs over, covering the yard.

As her cries cease, mine begin. I have seen other slaughters but this one will stay with me.

VI

My grandmother's verandah before they renovated the house sloped downhill. The direction the marbles took as they rolled toward the set-up dominoes was always the same. There was a particular lizard at one end, who crawled up to take the sun in the afternoon. I provoked him, knowing he had a temper since half his tail was missing. As he got angry he turned black with rage and blew a balloon of flesh from his throat—and sat there.

VII

Sitting in the maid's room asking her about her daughter, who is somewhere else. I examine the contents of her dressing table: perfume, comb, hand-mirror, romantic comics, missal.

The maid is sunning rectangles of white cloth on the bushes behind the house. I ask her what they are. She mutters something and moves off. They are bright with whiteness and soft to the touch. I suspect they are a private matter and ask no more about them.

VIII

The river—as I know it—runs from a dam at my cousins' sugar mill down to a pool at the bottom.

On Monday the women make their way to the river, balancing zinc washtubs on a braided cloth on their heads—this cloth has an African name. They take their places at specific rocks and rub, beat, wet, wring, and spread their laundry in the sun. And then leave. The rocks are streaked white after their chore is finished.

This is *our* land, *our* river—I have been told. So when women wash their clothes above the place where I swim; when the butcher's wife cleans tripe on Saturday morning; when a group of boys I do not know are using *my* pool—I hate them for taking up *my* space.

I hate them for taking up space; I hate them for not including me.

IX

The butcher's wife—after she has cleaned the tripe—comes to wax the parlor floor. She has a daughter my age who today is embarrassed and angry: I think it is because she is wearing one of my old dresses.

(Twenty years later I find she is part of us: "from" my great-uncle.)

There are many mysterious births here.

Three people come up to the steps and ask for my grandfather (who by this time is almost dead). I am suspicious and question them closely. My grandmother explains: "They are your grandfather's *outside* children."

X

Three women—sisters, my second cousins; unmarried; middle-aged—live across the river. They have a plant called "Midnight Mystery" on their verandah. They come late one night to fetch me and we walk down the path, our way lit by a small boy with a bottle lamp. We balance ourselves across the river and reach the house—in time to see the large white flower unfold.

XI

One reason the parlor floor is waxed on Saturday is that my grandmother holds church on Sunday. People arrive at nine and sit for two hours: giving testimony, singing hymns, reading scripture. They sip South African wine and eat squares of white bread.

Religion looms: Zinc roofs rock on Sunday morning.

XII

The river "comes down": the dam breaks; rocks shift; animals are carried along.

The clouds build across the mountains and move into our valley. Then it rains. Over the rain I can hear the noise of the river. It *is* a roar; even the gully, which pays the river tribute, roars—and becomes dangerous.

This is clear power.

XIII

We cook on a woodstove in a kitchen behind the house. Our water is taken from the river in brimming kerosene tins. We read by lamp and moon light.

XIV

On one hillside next to the house is the coffee piece: the bushes are low, with dark-green leaves and dark-red fruit. Darkness informs the place. Darkness and damp. Tall trees preserve the dark. Things hide here.

I pick coffee for my grandmother. To be gentle is important: the bushes are sensitive. I carefully fill my basket with the fruit.

XV

After the birth of each of my grandmother's five children the cord was buried and orange trees planted near the house. These trees now bear the names of her children.

XVI

One child died—a son, at eighteen. His grave is in the flower garden, shaded by the orange trees. She tends the grave often, singing "What a Friend We Have in Jesus."

The walls of my grandmother's parlor are decorated with two photographs: of her two remaining sons.

XVII

My mother is my grandmother's daughter. My acquaintance with my mother in this house is from the schoolbooks stored in boxes underneath. Worms have tunneled the pages, the covers are crossed with mold—making the books appear ancient. She has left me to find her here, under this house: I seek identity in a childish hand and obsolete geography.

XVIII

A madwoman steals my grandfather's horse and tries to ride away. I know several madwomen here. She is the boldest; riding bareback, naked. The others walk up and down, talking to themselves and others. One talks to a lizard in the cashew tree at the bottom of the yard. Another sits in the river, refusing to cross.

This woman—one of my cousins—tells me twenty years later about her terror of leaving her place; about the shock treatments the family arranges in town; about how she kept the accounts; about her sister's slow death and how she cared for her.

It must have meant something that all those mad were women. The men were called idiots (an accident of birth)—or drunks.

The women's madness was ascribed to several causes: childlessness, celibacy, "change": such was the nature of their naive science.

XIX

An old woman who sometimes works for us has built a house by the roadside. It is built of clay—from the roadbed—with wood for structure. It has a thatch roof and rests on cement blocks. It is one-room.

She promises to make me a cake if I help her paper the walls. I arrive early, my arms filled with newspapers. We mix flour paste and seek suitable stories for decoration. Pleased with our results, we gather flowers and put them in gourds around the room. True to her word, she bakes me a cake in an empty condensed milk tin.

XX

Walking down to the shop by the railway crossing, saying good morning, people stop me and ask for my mother—often mistaking me for her.

XXI

I want to visit my mother's school where she broke her ankle playing cricket and used the books which now lie under the house. I can't get to the school but I play cricket; using a carved bamboo root as she did and the dried stalk of a coconut tree for a bat. I play on the same pitch she used—a flat protected place across the road.

XXII

Walking through the water and over the rocks, I am exploring the river—eating bitter susumba and sweet Valencia oranges. Up past pools named for people who drowned there; to the dam; to the sugar mill where I get wet sugar.

XXIII

What is here for me: where do these things lead:
warmth
light
wet sugar
rain and river water
earth
the wood fire
distance
slaughter
mysterious births
fertility
the women at the river
my grandmother's authority with land and scripture
a tree named with my mother's name.

Twenty years these things rush back at me: the memories of a child inside and outside.

XXIV

Behind the warmth and light are dark and damp/behind the wet sugar, cane fields/behind the rain and river water, periods of drought/underneath the earth are the dead/underneath the wood fire are ashes to be emptied/underneath the distance is separation/underneath the slaughter is hunger/behind the mysterious births is my own/behind the fertility are the verdicts of insanity/behind the women at the river are earlier women/underlying my grandmother's authority with land and scripture is obedience to a drunken husband/under a tree named with my mother's name is a rotted cord.

Against Granite

It is a marble building—but like a cave inside.

In the basement—against granite—a woman sits in plain sight. She is black: and old. "Are you a jazz singer?" someone asks. "No—a historian."

Archives are spread on the table where she works: complicated statistics of imprisonment; plans of official edifices; physiognomic studies of the type.

She is writing a history of incarceration.

Here is where black women congregate—against granite. This is their headquarters; where they write history. Around tables they exchange facts—details of the unwritten past. Like the women who came before them—the women they are restoring to their work/space—the historians are skilled at unraveling lies; are adept at detecting the reality beneath the erasure.

Out back is evidence of settlement: a tin roof crests a hill amid mountains—orange and tangerine trees form a natural border. A river where women bathe can be seen from the historians' enclave. The land has been cultivated; the crops are ready for harvest. In the foreground a young black woman sits on grass which flourishes. Here women pick freely from the trees.

(This is all in the primary line of vision. Not peripheral, but plain.)

Around the periphery are those who would
enforce silence:
slicers/suturers/invaders/abusers/sterilizers/infibulators/
castrators/dividers/enclosers

traditional technicians/technicians of tradition.

Those who practice on women/those who practice
     on children:
The providers of Depo-provera:
     the deprivers of women's lives.
The promoters of infant formula:
     the dealers in child-death.
The purveyors of starvation and mutilation—there is no way
else to say it.

Because peripheral, the border guards are shadowy—their
features indistinct. They wear no uniforms, only name-tags:
Upjohn, Nestle, Riker's, Welfare, Rockland State, Jesus, the
Law of the Land—and yes, and also—Gandhi and Kenyatta.

The historians—like those who came before them—mean to
survive. But know they may not. They know that though
shadowy, the border guards have influence, and carry danger
with them. And with this knowledge, the women manage.

And in the presence of this knowledge the historians plant,
weed, hoe, raise houses, sew, and wash—and continue their
investigations: into the one-shot contraceptive; the slow
deaths of their children; the closing-up of vulvas and the
cutting-out of tongues. By opening the sutures, applying
laundry soap and brown sugar, they draw out the poisons and
purify the wounds. And maintain vigilance to lessen the
possiblity of reinfection.

Each evening at dusk, the women gather under the tin roof
which shelters the meeting-house: the progress notes of the
day's work are read—then they cook dinner, talk, and sing: old
songs whose noise carries a long distance.

A History of Costume

In the foreground a bird with a beautiful plume circles
round and round as if lost or giddy. There are red holes
in its head where there should be eyes. Another bird,
tied to a stake, writhes incessantly, for red ants devour
it. Both are decoys. . . . It is in the nesting season that
the plumes are brightest, so, if we wish to go on making
pictures, we must imagine innumerable mouths open-
ing and shutting, until—as no parent bird comes to
feed them—the young birds rot where they sit. Then
there are the wounded birds, trailing leg or wing, as
they flutter off to droop or falter in the dust. But
perhaps the most unpleasant sight that we must make
ourselves imagine is the sight of the bird tightly held in
one hand while another pierces the eyeballs with a
feather. But these hands—are they the hands of men
or of women?

> Virginia Woolf, "The Plumage Bill,"
> *The Woman's Leader,* July 23, 1920

In the basement of the museum finery is on display; a history of
costume, open to the public. Plaster models—their heads
swathed in varicolored nylon stockings—are placed in rooms
dedicated to periods of time.

I

My mother and I meet in public places—and move between
the swathed heads:
the faceless heads and covered bodies
the covered faces, the emblazoned bodies
the paisley-shawled bodies
cut off from
the undistinguished heads.

We came to this exhibit in part to connect, in part to recollect, but we hold few memories in common; and our connections are limited by silences between us. Our common ground is the island where we were born—and we speak in the language spoken there. And we bear a close resemblance, except for eye-color.

II

We move into a room
filled with
    fans
    corsets
    parasols
    shoes
the covering of birds/the perimeters of whales/handles made from the tusks of elephants/the work of the silkworm: to receive the lotusfoot.

The tiny shoes are lush: carefully designed,
    painstakingly executed.
Green silk bordered in red,
    embroidered with golden birds in flight.
Sewn perhaps by a mother for her daughter,
    according to custom.
And according to custom, also,
    fitted by that mother over time.

III

I start to talk about these feet, but our conversation slides into another room, where a court dress of the eighteenth century is displayed: lapis blue silk sewn with silver; cinched waist; hips spread outward supported by a cage; breasts suggested by slight plaster mounds; small hands gesture toward the throat—no legs are visible.

Behind this dress is a painting: Adélaïde Labille-Guiard—*Portrait of the Artist with Two Pupils* (1785). The artist is at the center of the composition, before a canvas; two students stand behind her, women. The artist, later absorbed into silence, meant this work to show her dedication to teaching women; devised a state plan for female education. And her work, because of her intent, was considered radical and dangerous.

I want to talk about this woman's work, but the painting hangs here because of what she wears; and this is what my mother notices.

IV

These rooms are crowded—with artificial light, canned music—women wander past the work of women become the trappings of women. Which women turned the birds-of-paradise into a knee-length frock?—the life-work of creatures worn during one evening. By whose direction? Who trapped the birds? What decoys were employed? Who killed them?

V

In a corner of one room are enormous ornamental combs. From a wall an etching mocks as women topple—fooled into imbalance. But look again: It is the women-alone who fall. At the left, serenely upright, a woman walks supported by a man; at the right a deliveryman hurries, a gigantic package carried on his head.

Together my mother and I remember women with filled market baskets; women who carry a week's wet laundry from the washing place; a woman we know who bears water on her head—each day for half a mile. And briefly—recalling the women of our common ground—we meet.

VI

And then the wigs: the hair of another woman. Jo's chestnut hair cut off. The plumage of an ostrich. To wear another woman's hair. To wear the feathers of a large flightless bird. To cover a head with hair that has been sold.

The women of Marie Antoinette's court: their elevated heads—and the rats they say lived in them. We talk about teased hair; knotted, split, sprayed hair; bleached, dyed, kinked, straightened, curled hair. My mother's hair streaked blonde.

VII

Inevitably we change places with the displays: How did they sit? How did they walk? How did they get their waists so small?

We see ourselves in riding habits: black velvet coat with thick red roses—the jacket of Queen Alexandra; heavily veiled top hat; high leather boots and slender crop—seated askew, the body placed to one side. Would we slide off? Would we use the whip? The first time—would we wash the blood off, or let it fade?

VIII

In a dimly lit room are camisoles, slips, all other underthings: these are soft cotton, pale flowers embroidered and connected with gentle pastel ribbons. I imagine women dressing and undressing—together in their white eyelet cotton camisoles, helping each other undo the ribbons. Perhaps napping during the afternoon of a nineteenth-century house party—lying side by side on large pillows, briefly released. Perhaps touching; stroking the ribcage bruised by stays; applying a hanky dipped in bay rum to the temples of another. Perhaps kissing her forehead after the application is done, perhaps taking her hand. Head on another's shoulder, drifting. To be waked too soon. I like to think of women making soft underclothes for their comfort—as they comfort each other.

IX

This dream is interrupted by the crimson silk pajamas of a harem woman: purple brocade coat trimmed in gold braid and galloon; coins suspended above her eyes.

X

This meeting-place is filled with stolen gold, silver, coral, pearls; with plundered skins, shells, bones, and teeth. Aspects of ornamental bondage, all used to maintain the costume.

XI

We reach the end of the exhibit: in a corner (American, nineteenth century) are a mourning couple; mother and daughter in identical black garb, the head of the mother swathed in black net; the tragedy of bombazine on a five-year-old likeness holding her mother's mourning hands.

Claiming an Identity
They Taught Me to Despise

"Was anyone in this class not born in the United States?" the teacher asked us in the fifties. I was in third grade. I stood up and mumbled, "Jamaica," and became the focus of their scrutiny. I filled their silence with rapid lies.

Still in the third grade, I am kept after school for talking. My mother—young and thin, a pale gray coat which falls from squared-off shoulders, her brown hair long and turned under at her neck—comes to fetch me. As she confronts the teacher I begin to cry, my guilt and shame at bringing her into this strange place overcomes me.

I want to protect her from their scrutiny and what they will never understand.

I

> Bertha! Bertha! The wind caught my hair and it streamed outward like wings. It might bear me up, I thought, if I jumped to those hard stones.
>
> Jean Rhys, *Wide Sargasso Sea*

> Grace Poole gave him a cord, and he pinioned [her arms] behind her: with more rope, which was at hand, he bound her to a chair.
>
> Charlotte Brontë, *Jane Eyre*

pinion: the distal part of a bird's wing, including the carpus, the metacarpus, the phalanges; a wing—*as a noun.*

pinion: to cut off the pinion of a wing to prevent flight; to disable or restrain by binding the wings or arms, especially close to the body; to bind the wings or arms of; to shackle; to confine—*as a verb.*

To imagine I am the sister of Bertha Rochester. We are the remainders of slavery—residue:
>   white cockroaches
>   white niggers
>   quadroons
>   octoroons
>   mulattos
>   creoles
>   white niggers.

Her hair became wings with the interference of the wind. And she smashed *on those hard stones.* Did the sockets pain her as *he bound her to a chair* with his swift and assured grasp? And Grace Poole, the alcoholic female keeper: what were her thoughts?

Pressed into service, moved into the great house—
>   early on.
Daughters of the masters/whores of the masters
At one with the great house/
>   at odds with the great house
Setting fire to the great house/the masters/
>   sometimes ourselves.

Early on I worried about children. Tales of throwback were common. Tell-tale hair, thick noses and heavy mouths—you could be given away so easily. Better remain unbred.

II

>   *creole:* (the Fr. form of *criollo,* a West Indian, probably
>   a negro corruption of the Span. *criadillo,* the dim. of
>   *criado,* one bred or reared, from *criar,* to breed, a
>   derivative of the Lat. *creare,* to create.). . . It is now
>   used of the descendants of non-aboriginal races born
>   and settled in the West Indies, in various parts of the
>   American mainland, and in Mauritius, Réunion, and
>   some other places colonized by Spain, Portugal, France,
>   or. . .by England. . . . The use of the word by some
>   writers as necessarily implying a person of mixed
>   blood is totally erroneous; in itself "creole" has no
>   distinction of colour; a creole may be a person of
>   European, negro, or mixed extraction—or even a
>   horse. . . . The difference in type between the creoles
>   and the European races from which they have sprung,
>   a difference often considerable, is due principally to
>   changed environment—especially to the tropical or
>   semi-tropical climate of the lands they inhabit.
>
>   *Encyclopedia Britannica,* 11th edition

They can always fall back on the landscape—the sudden
storms—the sun which burns even as it warms. The *changed
environment* of red dirt, volcanic sand, sea-eggs whose spikes
wash out with piss. Alligators. Jellyfish. Oysters who cling to
pilings, to be sliced off with the sharp stroke of the *machete.*
The high grass of sugar cane etching fine lines into bare legs.
The extravagant blossoms which release strange aromas into
the too-warm air. The bright moonlight spun with these
perfumes. These are their clichés—a thin film covering the
real.

To imagine I am the sister of Annie Palmer
    "white witch"
    creole bitch
    imported to the north coast of Jamaica
    legend of the island
    mistress of Rose Hall
    guilty of husband-murder three times over.

We drove past Rose Hall often when I was a child. They repeated her life to me. They indicated the three coconut trees she used for grave-markers. They told me she practiced *obeah* and drank the whitemen's blood for power and slept with the black overseer who killed her for infidelity.

And a rich Jamaican family bought the staircase where she died and instructed their servants not to wash the blood off.

My blood commenced early. The farther back you go the thicker it becomes. And the mother is named the link, the carrier—the source of the Nile. Did she attend each birth with caution? Waiting to see the degree of our betrayal?

"Pork!" the streetcleaner called.
Pigskin scraped clean.
"You not us. You not them either."

III

I find a broadside from nineteenth-century America. The statement: *a creole may be. . .even a horse* is illuminated.

RAFFLE

    Mr. Joseph Jennings respectfully informs his friends and the public that, at the request of many acquaintances, he has been induced to purchase from Mr. Osborne of Missouri, the celebrated **Dark Bay Horse, "Star,"** aged five years, square trotter and warranted sound: with a new light Trotting Buggy and Harness. Also the dark, stout **Mulatto Girl, "Sarah,"** aged about twenty years, general house servant, valued at *nine hundred dollars,* and guaranteed, and **will be raffled for** at 4 o'clock p.m., February first, at the selection hotel of the subscribers. The above is as represented and those persons who may wish to engage in the usual practice of raffling, will, I assure them, be perfectly satisfied with their destiny in this affair.

They name us. They buy us and sell us.

I am twenty-two and sitting in my mother's kitchen. She is about to inform me "officially." I question her delay. "I didn't think it mattered"—as if to say, "I didn't think you'd mind." "You don't know what it was like when we first came here. No one wanted to be colored. Your father's family was always tracing me. And these Americans, they just don't understand. My cousin was fired from her job in a department store when they found out she was passing. I stopped seeing her because your father was always teasing me about my colored cousin. Things are different now. You're lucky you look the way you do, you could get any man. Anyone says anything to you, tell them your father's white."

IV

I wish to stay here in the dark. . .where I belong.

Wide Sargasso Sea

I dreamed there was a record album called *Black Women.* The front of the album was a baroque painting depicting a galleon on rough seas—sailing over a dragon which was visible on either side of the bow. Inset was the portrait of a large light-skinned woman—in a white turban and plain white bodice: dressed as a slave. This woman was also at the helm of the galleon and was identified in fine writing as the first black navigator. The painting, the writing continued, had been taken from a manuscript entitled *Emergam,* Munich, 1663. The dream continued—I interviewed two white women historians who told me the manuscript had been proved a fake. We argued about the false and the real but they were adamant.

(*Emergam* is the first-person future of the Latin verb *emergere:* to rise up, emerge, free oneself.)

V

> These pictures were in watercolours. The first repre-sented clouds low and livid, rolling over a swollen sea: all the distance was in eclipse; so too was the foregound; or, rather, the nearest billows, for there was no land. One gleam of light lifted into relief a half-submerged mast, on which sat a cormorant, dark and large, with wings flecked with foam; its beak held a gold bracelet, set with gems. . .a drowned corpse glanced through the green water; a fair arm was the only limb clearly visible, whence the bracelet had been washed or torn.
>
> *Jane Eyre*

This is the vision of Jane Eyre, small and pale. She is speaking of us. We dwell in the penumbra of the eclipse. In the half-darkness. They tell us the dark and light lie beyond us. "I feel sorry for you," the dark woman said. "You don't know who you are."

The ship in the vision has foundered. The cormorant has taken her place and surveys the damage. Her dark plumage is wet, so we know who has taken the bracelet from the white woman's arm. *The large dark bird sits with wings pinioned in the wooden chair.*

It would seem the cormorant has replaced the dragon in my dream: but no, she is the navigator, expressed by another, stripped of her power. She nests on high and dives deep into warm waters. She has green eyes and is long-lived. (It came down to this: my eyes might save me. Green-blue. Almost blue. Changing with each costume.)

VI

I have seen the wreckage of sugar mills covered with damp and green mosses. When the concrete cracks across, green veins trace the damage. There are tracks where mules used to circle, to crush the cane. There are copper cauldrons once used to boil the juice, from which molasses and foam were drawn off to make rum. (The purest rum—do I have to say it?—is colorless and called white. Other rum is colored artifically, taking on the darkness of the casks over time—they think the golden tint makes it more appealing. The final type is colored by impurities and was once called Negro rum.)

There are great houses throughout this island abandoned to the forest.

A great aunt keeps a chipped crystal doorknob—a solid polyhedron—on the dining table of her pensioner's flat in England. "From our place at Dry Harbour," she explains. "Fancy. . .every door had one."

Wetness spreads through the wooden house. Damp spots emerge through French wallpaper where children spin thin hoops along gravel walkways. And women glide with frilled umbrellas. This is not part of us: this nineteenth-century scene of well-being. Better to look in the shacks built in the back, where newsprint covered the walls. And calendars advertised the English royal family.

VII

The white-haired woman sits with rice piled on her dinner plate. I am ten years old and we are visiting a branch of the family. She is my first encounter with the island I left when I was three. She is the first encounter I remember. "More rice!" she screams at the woman who serves the table. And rice is brought. "More rice!" again. My sister—who is six—and I giggle. There is a woman at the head of the table who screams for rice. The mound is high. The grains slide down the mound and onto the white cloth. "No more rice," she closes.

VIII

> You are trying to make me into someone else, calling me by another name. I know, that's *obeah* too.
>
> *Wide Sargasso Sea*

The Alms House at May Pen is yellowing wood. It stands above a long flight of wooden steps with a narrow handrail. There is—whenever we pass—a crowd at the top of the stairs, gathered in the yard of the Alms House. I always ask about these people. Somewhere I have confused them with lepers. "Are they lepers?" I ask my father. "No, not lepers; just people with no place to go."

The Garden

I

Not a walled place—in fact, open on all sides.
Not secret—but private.
A private open space.

I trim the stakes to mark the rows—string a fence with cord to support the snow peas—move rocks aside and bits of porcelain, some plastic; each day there is more to be taken away. Carefully dig to the required depth for broccoli, lettuces—turn the eyes of limas and string beans downward—mix the thin seeds of carrots with sturdy radishes: "companionate planting"—one protects the other. Basil alongside tomato. Garlic everywhere.

The man across the way, busy with his machine, cigarette ash mixing with turned earth—is watching me. I am wearing khaki shorts and a t-shirt which reads Xantippe. He approaches, smiling, rolling across the border. "Do you want me to go through with my rototiller?" he asks. I concentrate on the old hoe I found in the barn, and respond only after I have made contact with the furrow. "No, thank you, I prefer to work by hand." A smirk, then—"Anytime you change your mind. . ." drifting off.

At first I didn't notice. But then a large footprint made me look further. His mark across the rows I had made yesterday. One enormous foot planted on a squash hill. And the traces of his mechanical sidekick zigzagging over lettuce, broccoli, chard. "I could kill," my only thought.

II

"I sometimes attack the ground, rather than moving in a smooth rhythm. When I garden, which is almost daily, I think at least once of my mother's challenge that everything will probably die, and so it's my challenge to assure that everything lives—my difficulty in thinning, *sentimental obstacle*. This goes to a deep place; to being told I was unloving and unnurturing as a child (and adult). I feel the weeds in the garden encroaching as a personal threat to my ability to nurture. I also feel them as my mother and sister encroaching on my life; so the plants become a metaphor for my own life and the powerful weeds (which seem to be able to endure anything) my mother's and sister's demands. So my gardening is a pitched battle against this; and is thus contaminated. I have also felt as I walk to the garden (in the middle of a meadow) that I am threatened; that there is a snake or animal lurking somewhere—that someday I will see this creature, and the garden will be spoiled.

"Last night, reading about Florence Nightingale—her final method to save herself from the unending encroachments of her mother and sister was to be ill. She had tried for many years to rid herself of their constant and insistent presence in and demands on her life. She never confronted the need for separation and worked through it. What she did was to remove herself from them by (1) working herself almost to the point of death; ridding them, by filling her life and mind with other matters, which could not have possibly interested them (yet she admittedly longed for her mother's approval); and (2) when this was not successful, by becoming ill every time they threatened to come near, thus punishing herself also. . . . And so I woke this morning with a pinched nerve in my neck and my right arm numb. Partly physical, of course, but I am experiencing it as a knot of unexpressed anger which I have turned against myself—another implosive reaction, like depression. The conception of Nightingale by her mother and sister was so similar to my own experience: autocratic, aloof, puritanical, unloving, willing to devote her life to 'strangers' rather than to 'family,' deviant, etc.

"How they 'accidentally' shut her pet owl, Athena, in the attic and killed her—and how they taunted Nightingale for loving her owl more than she loved them."

(This was written about another garden.)

III

The rakish stripes of the potato bugs—hard back crushing under a stone. Dull gray shell of the squash borer—smashing one with two fingers, and thick blue milk oozes forth. Bright orange eggs fast to the underside of eggplant leaves, scraped off with a fingernail. Japanese beetles plop into a coffee tin filled with turpentine. Green cabbage worms succumb to a dusting of wood ash. And tiny white flies scatter as a mist of water and red pepper reaches them.

The books I use call these "natural controls." Still I fear that this hand-to-hand combat will be punished.

IV

The fleshy placenta of the bean-seed breaks the surface.

An article in the newspaper: a child with spina bifida—open spine. Thoughts of Susannah and her open-heart surgery. A child with Downs syndrome and a defective valve. Time spent with her and a desire to give myself over to her enormous needs totally—playing the *Red Back Book* for hours while she rocked in a corner and twirled her piece of silk. Each time the record finished—a scream. Also knowing the reality of her existence and how it is for her mother to have a child like her plus two other children. But she is the only kind of child I can imagine for myself. How she learned my name and slept with me—nose running on the quilt. I have no children and know I never will.

V

Ice crystals still in the grass.
The translucent skin of green tomatoes.
Squashes suspended.
It seems as if the plants drip—
an early frost.

Cutting back the leaves and stems of the basil plants—string beans—pea vines. Laying them on the compost heap—now that decomposition has begun. This is a strange destruction.

Women gone mad from childlessness—the philosophers talk about unfulfilled purpose—stray uterus rampaging—burning, cutting, slicing—discarding. *Immanence* and *inner space.* Our universe—the black hole—the void within.

VI

I dream about my mother and sister. Both about to give birth. In a dark hospital staircase my mother hands me an enameled bowl—containing a piece of tissue and some blood. Not an abortion, not even a miscarriage—a child who will develop according to my care. My sister sits back, full belly stroked, while the tissue is delivered to me—in my care. I intentionally neglect it—letting it drown in its own piss.

VII

A history of women and gardens:
Dorothea Lange's ex-slave with a long memory. Dickinson kneeling on her folded red blanket, tending exotica. Fannie Lou

Hamer standing in a cotton field. The Chrisman sisters before their sod house. Sibylla Merian escaping to Surinam to draw from life.

And Millet's *gleaners* and Raphael's *belle jardinière* and Wordsworth's *solitary reaper.*

Market women in Jamaica, baskets hung across a donkey's back while they walk alongside—a stick in hand to urge the animal on—to Linstead, to May Pen, to Port Maria. Hair spun into braids under a straw hat, tight black eyes of ackees stare from raffia pods—fresh dress—sneakers newly whitened. To sit or squat for hours while they teach about their work.

My own grandmother: "I was very glad hearing from you again, because your last letter said you intended to live in the country, it's nice that you feel more safe there, and you can plant your things and watch them growing. That's what I always do when I was younger, I loved to plant and see them growing, now I am old I can't do these things anymore and besides there is no land room, your uncle has the whole place in citrus."

VII

In this cold the spinach may bolt.
The broccoli continue.
The turnips fulfill their globes underground.

IX

To garden is a solitary act.

Travel Notes

I wanted to be the lone figure on the landscape.
The cat burglar passing silent in the night.
The fast driver—unaffiliated—unnoticed.
This is not how it is.

Sometimes I see a small house—sometimes shacks attract me.
I wonder how it would be to live hidden.

I am standing in the doorway of the dining room at Haworth
Parsonage. *My sister Emily loved the moors. . . . Out of a sullen
hollow in a livid hill-side, her mind could make an Eden.* —I
stare at the horsehair sofa where Emily Brontë died.

Outside are the thousands of graves. Wind and rain obscuring
the vision. Mosses cross the outer walls.

While inside glass cases display the tiny notebooks filled with
stories. The needlework of the sisters.

Downstairs is the souvenir kiosk. The portraits of Keeper,
Grasper, the hawk Hero. Views of the moors—heather—gorse.
Top Withens. Kitchen. Churchyard. *She found in the bleak
solitude many and dear delights; and not the least and best-
loved was—liberty. Liberty was the breath of Emily's nostrils.*

Across from this kiosk is a bulletin board advising women of the existence of the Yorkshire Ripper and the necessity that we remain indoors.

The North Wind demolished their already weakened lungs—Anne and Emily. Charlotte died of pregnancy. Branwell of opium and drink. The old man of old age. Much earlier a mother and two other sisters: cancer, consumption, typhoid.

Back home—I find a suspect has been caught. He kept to himself. He was a shy man. He and his wife had no children. The police have his wife under guard. There are threats on her life.

"But we already know that women are oppressed," the student said to me. "I had hoped this course would deal with something else."

How do we keep their attention?
Our own.

As a child I saved maps. Haunted airports. Begged for travel brochures and posters of bazaars and castles. I wanted to go overseas. Always looked forward.

Traveling through my own time I often look back.

I am in Brighton where England's Neo-Nazis have head-quarters. Where Fanny Imlay—Wollstonecraft's daughter—killed herself, wearing her mother's watch and undergarment.

Brighton is an hour from Lewes—where Virginia Woolf walked into the River Ouse. I think about a memoir written by Woolf's cook—Louie Mayer—how she described the last afternoon: as Virginia wandered through the garden, bumping into branches. And Leonard suggested Virginia dust—but she lost interest.

These details crowd me.

What is left of Wollstonecraft's grave is a plaque by King's Cross Station.

In King's Cross once I saw a woman in the ladies' room—a large naked white woman accompanied by her belongings. She was standing in a corner against a wall, calmly washing herself. Wetting and soaping and drying herself with brown paper.

Other women came and went.

As a child I pressed my fingers against my closed eyes— watched the stars, planets, comets, and meteorites move against them. As if I could contain the universe behind my eyelids.

It is the anniversary of the first imprisonment of
     suffragists—
Annie Kenney and Cristabel Pankhurst.
Someone has left a bouquet of irises—purple
tied with ribbon—green:
the colors of the movement.

These lie in front of Emmeline Pankhurst's statue which stands to the side of the Houses of Parliament. The note attached to the bouquet is in a strong and older hand—perhaps of a woman who actually remembers 1905. The ink runs in the drizzle.

Now the meaning of green ribbon has shifted. They are killing Black children in Atlanta—also elsewhere. Georgia Dean, a retired factory worker, suggests wearing an inverted V of green—the color of growing things.

Each newspaper report seems more clouded than before: today they claimed the children died at the hands of a "gentle" killer: does this translate as female? homosexual?

What are they getting at?

The Mark of the Beast—a special issue on the Klan. On the cover a member clasps a child; his eyes seem hollowed—the child's, I mean—the member is a woman.

I meet two women in Texas—they live on a farm in a small town north of Austin. Outside their kitchen is a pile of rocks where their cat stares down a diamondback.

They prepare a noose of cord—slide one rock back. The diamondback raises her head to strike. They slide the noose around her neck.

She stretches to her length. "Four feet of solid muscle"—one woman explains.

They place the snake in a garbage can—secure its lid by rope.

There is another snake in the rockpile—then another.

"We're lucky we had seven cans," says one woman—and a pickup to drive the diamondbacks twenty-five miles away and let them go: one by one.

A solid day's work.

If I Could Write This in Fire, I Would Write This in Fire

I

We were standing under the waterfall at the top of Orange River. Our chests were just beginning to mound—slight hills on either side. In the center of each were our nipples, which were losing their sideways look and rounding into perceptible buttons of dark flesh. Too fast it seemed. We touched each other, then, quickly and almost simultaneously, raised our arms to examine the hairs growing underneath. Another sign. Mine was wispy and light-brown. My friend Zoe had dark hair curled up tight. In each little patch the riverwater caught the sun so we glistened.

The waterfall had come about when my uncles dammed up the river to bring power to the sugar mill. Usually, when I say "sugar mill" to anyone not familiar with the Jamaican country-side or for that matter my family, I can tell their minds cast an image of tall smokestacks, enormous copper cauldrons, a man in a broad-brimmed hat with a whip, and several dozens of slaves—that is, if they have any idea of how large sugar mills once operated. It's a grandiose expression—like plantation, verandah, out-building. (Try substituting farm, porch, outside toilet.) To some people it even sounds romantic.

Our sugar mill was little more than a round-roofed shed, which contained a wheel and woodfire. We paid an old man to run it, tend the fire, and then either bartered or gave the sugar away, after my grandmother had taken what she needed. Our canefield was about two acres of flat land next to the river. My grandmother had six acres in all—one donkey, a mule, two cows, some chickens, a few pigs, and stray dogs and cats who had taken up residence in the yard.

Her house had four rooms, no electricity, no running water. The kitchen was a shed in the back with a small pot-bellied stove. Across from the stove was a mahogany counter, which had a white enamel basin set into it. The only light source was a window, a small space covered partly by a wooden shutter. We washed our faces and hands in enamel bowls with cold water carried in kerosene tins from the river and poured from enamel pitchers. Our chamber pots were enamel also, and in the morning we carefully placed them on the steps at the side of the house where my grandmother collected them and disposed of their contents. The outhouse was about thirty yards from the back door—a "closet" as we called it—infested with lizards capable of changing color. When the door was shut it was totally dark, and the lizards made their presence known by the noise of their scurrying through the torn newspaper, or the soft shudder when they dropped from the walls. I remember most clearly the stench of the toilet, which seemed to hang in the air in that climate.

But because every little piece of reality exists in relation to another little piece, our situation was not that simple. It was to our yard that people came with news first. It was in my grandmother's parlor that the Disciples of Christ held their meetings.

Zoe lived with her mother and sister on borrowed ground in a place called Breezy Hill. She and I saw each other almost every day on our school vacations over a period of three years. Each morning early—as I sat on the cement porch with my coffee cut with condensed milk—she appeared: in her straw hat, school tunic faded from blue to gray, white blouse, sneakers hanging around her neck. We had coffee together, and a piece of hard-dough bread with butter and cheese, waited a bit and headed for the river. At first we were shy with each other. We did not start from the same place.

There was land. My grandparents' farm. And there was color.

(My family was called *red*. A term which signified a degree of whiteness. "We's just a flock of red people," a cousin of mine said once.) In the hierarchy of shades I was considered among the lightest. The countrywomen who visited my grandmother commented on my "tall" hair—meaning long. Wavy, not curly.

I had spent the years from three to ten in New York and spoke—at first—like an American. I wore American clothes: shorts, slacks, bathing suit. Because of my American past I was looked upon as the creator of games. Cowboys and Indians. Cops and Robbers. Peter Pan.

(While the primary colonial identification for Jamaicans was English, American colonialism was a strong force in my childhood—and of course continues today. We were sent American movies and American music. American aluminum companies had already discovered bauxite on the island and were shipping the ore to their mainland. United Fruit bought our bananas. White Americans came to Montego Bay, Ocho Rios, and Kingston for their vacations and their cruise ships docked in Port Antonio and other places. In some ways America was seen as a better place than England by many Jamaicans. The farm laborers sent to work in American agribusiness came home with dollars and gifts and new clothes; there were few who mentioned American racism. Many of the middle class who emigrated to Brooklyn or Staten

Island or Manhattan were able to pass into the white American world—saving their blackness for other Jamaicans or for trips home; in some cases, forgetting it altogether. Those middle-class Jamaicans who could not pass for white managed differently—not unlike the Bajans in Paule Marshall's *Brown Girl, Brownstones*—saving, working, investing, buying property. Completely separate in most cases from Black Americans.)

I was someone who had experience with the place that sent us triple features of B-grade westerns and gangster movies. And I had tall hair and light skin. And I was the granddaughter of my grandmother. So I had power. I was the cowboy, Zoe was my sidekick, the boys we knew were Indians. I was the detective, Zoe was my "girl," the boys were the robbers. I was Peter Pan, Zoe was Wendy Darling, the boys were the lost boys. And the terrain around the river—jungled and dark green—was Tombstone, or Chicago, or Never-Never Land.

This place and my friendship with Zoe never touched my life in Kingston. We did not correspond with each other when I left my grandmother's home.

I never visited Zoe's home the entire time I knew her. It was a given: never suggested, never raised.

Zoe went to a state school held in a country church in Red Hills. It had been my mother's school. I went to a private all-girls school where I was taught by white Englishwomen and pale Jamaicans. In her school the students were caned as punishment. In mine the harshest punishment I remember was being sent to sit under the *lignum vitae* to "commune with nature." Some of the girls were out-and-out white (English and American), the rest of us were colored—only a few were dark. Our uniforms were blood-red gabardine, heavy and hot. Classes were held in buildings meant to recreate England:

damp with stone floors, facing onto a cloister, or quad as they called it. We began each day with the headmistress leading us in English hymns. The entire school stood for an hour in the zinc-roofed gymnasium.

Occasionally a girl fainted, or threw up. Once, a girl had a grand mal seizure. To any such disturbance the response was always "keep singing." While she flailed on the stone floor, I wondered what the mistresses would do. We sang "Faith of Our Fathers," and watched our classmate as her eyes rolled back in her head. I thought of people swallowing their tongues. This student was dark—here on a scholarship—and the only woman who came forward to help her was the gamesmistress, the only dark teacher. She kneeled beside the girl and slid the white web belt from her tennis shorts, clamping it between the girl's teeth. When the seizure was over, she carried the girl to a tumbling mat in a corner of the gym and covered her so she wouldn't get chilled.

Were the other women unable to touch this girl because of her darkness? I think that now. Her darkness and her scholarship. She lived on Windward Road with her grandmother; her mother was a maid. But darkness is usually enough for women like those to hold back. Then, we usually excused that kind of behavior by saying they were "ladies." (We were constantly being told we should be ladies also. One teacher went so far as to tell us many people thought Jamaicans lived in trees and we had to show these people they were mistaken.) In short, we felt insufficient to judge the behavior of these women. The English ones (who had the corner on power in the school) had come all this way to teach us. Shouldn't we treat them as the missionaries they were certain they were? The creole Jamaicans had a different role: they were passing on to those of us who were light-skinned the creole heritage of collaboration, assimilation, loyalty to our betters. We were expected to be willing subjects in this outpost of civilization.

The girl left school that day and never returned.

After prayers we filed into our classrooms. After classes we had games: tennis, field hockey, rounders (what the English call baseball), netball (what the English call basketball). For games we were divided into "houses"—groups named for Joan of Arc, Edith Cavell, Florence Nightingale, Jane Austen. Four white heroines. Two martyrs. One saint. Two nurses. (None of us knew then that there were Black women with Nightingale at Scutari.) One novelist. Three involved in whitemen's wars. Two dead in whitemen's wars. *Pride and Prejudice.*

Those of us in Cavell wore red badges and recited her last words before a firing squad in W. W. I: "Patriotism is not enough. I must have no hatred or bitterness toward anyone."

Sorry to say I grew up to have exactly that.

Looking back: To try and see when the background changed places with the foreground. To try and locate the vanishing point: where the lines of perspective converge and disappear. Lines of color and class. Lines of history and social context. Lines of denial and rejection. When did *we* (the light-skinned middle-class Jamaicans) take over for *them* as oppressors? I need to see when and how this happened. When what should have been reality was overtaken by what was surely unreality. When the house nigger became master.

"What's the matter with you? You think you're white or something?"
"Child, what you want to know 'bout Garvey for? The man was nothing but a damn fool."
"They not our kind of people."

Why did we wear wide-brimmed hats and try to get into Oxford? Why did we not return?

Great Expectations: a novel about origins and denial. about the futility and tragedy of that denial. about attempting assimilation. We learned this novel from a light-skinned Jamaican woman— she concentrated on what she called the "love affair" between Pip and Estella.

Looking back: Through the last page of *Sula.* "And the loss pressed down on her chest and came up into her throat. 'We was girls togehter,' she said as though explaining something." It was Zoe, and Zoe alone, I thought of. She snapped into my mind and I remembered no one else. Through the greens and blues of the riverbank. The flame of red hibiscus in front of my grandmother's house. The cracked grave of a former land-owner. The fruit of the ackee which poisons those who don't know how to prepare it.

"What is to become of us?"
We borrowed a baby from a woman and used her as our dolly. Dressed and undressed her. Dipped her in the riverwater. Fed her with the milk her mother had left with us: and giggled because we knew where the milk had come from.

A letter: "I am desperate. I need to get away. I beg you one fifty-dollar."

I send the money because this is what she asks for. I visit her on a trip back home. Her front teeth are gone. Her husband beats her and she suffers blackouts. I sit on her chair. She is given birth control pills which aggravate her "condition." We boil up sorrel and ginger. She is being taught by Peace Corps volunteers to embroider linen mats with little lambs on them and gives me one as a keepsake. We cool off the sorrel with a block of ice brought from the shop nearby. The shopkeeper immediately recognizes me as my grandmother's grand-daughter and refuses to sell me cigarettes. (I am twenty-seven.) We sit in the doorway of her house, pushing back the colored plastic strands which form a curtain, and talk about Babylon and Dred. About Manley and what he's doing for Jamaica. About how hard it is. We walk along the railway tracks—no longer used—to Crooked River and the post office. Her little daughter walks beside us and we recite a poem for her: "Mornin' buddy/Me no buddy fe wunna/Who den, den I saw?" and on and on.

I can come and go. And I leave. To complete my education in London.

II

Their goddam kings and their goddam queens. Grandmotherly Victoria spreading herself thin across the globe. Elizabeth II on our t.v. screens. We stop what we are doing. We quiet down. We pay our respects.

1981: In Massachusetts I get up at 5 a.m. to watch the royal wedding. I tell myself maybe the IRA will intervene. It's got to be better than starving themselves to death. Better to be a kamikaze in St. Paul's Cathedral than a hostage in Ulster. And last week Black and white people smashed storefronts all over the United Kingdom. But I really don't believe we'll see royal blood on t.v. I watch because they once ruled us. In the back of the cathedral a Maori woman sings an aria from Handel, and I notice that she is surrounded by the colored subjects.

To those of us in the commonwealth the royal family was the perfect symbol of hegemony. To those of us who were dark in the dark nations, the prime minister, the parliament barely existed. We believed in royalty—we were convinced in this belief. Maybe it played on some ancestral memories of West Africa—where other kings and queens had been. Altars and castles and magic.

The faces of our new rulers were everywhere in my childhood. Calendars, newsreels, magazines. Their presences were often among us. Attending test matches between the West Indians and South Africans. They were our landlords. Not always absentee. And no matter what Black leader we might elect— were we to choose independence—we would be losing something almost holy in our impudence.

WE ARE HERE BECAUSE YOU WERE THERE
BLACK PEOPLE AGAINST STATE BRUTALITY
BLACK WOMEN WILL NOT BE INTIMIDATED
WELCOME TO BRITAIN. . .WELCOME TO SECOND-CLASS CITIZENSHIP
(slogans of the Black movement in Britain)

Indian women cleaning the toilets in Heathrow airport. This is the first thing I notice. Dark women in saris trudging buckets back and forth as other dark women in saris—some covered by loosefitting winter coats—form a line to have their passports stamped.

The triangle trade: molasses/rum/slaves. Robinson Crusoe was on a slave-trading journey. Robert Browning was a mulatto. Holding pens. Jamaica was a seasoning station. Split tongues. Sliced ears. Whipped bodies. The constant pretense of civility against rape. Still. Iron collars. Tinplate masks. The latter a precaution: to stop the slaves from eating the sugar cane.

A pregnant woman is to be whipped—they dig a hole to accommodate her belly and place her face down on the ground. Many of us became light-skinned very fast. Traced ourselves through bastard lines to reach the duke of Devonshire. The earl of Cornwall. The lord of this and the lord of that. Our mothers' rapes were the thing unspoken.

You say: But Britain freed her slaves in 1833. Yes.

Tea plantations in India and Ceylon. Mines in Africa. The Cape-to-Cairo Railroad. Rhodes scholars. Suez Crisis. The whiteman's bloody burden. Boer War. Bantustans. Sitting in a theatre in London in the seventies. A play called *West of Suez*. A lousy play about British colonials. The finale comes when several well-known white actors are machine-gunned by several lesser-known Black actors. (As Nina Simone says: "This is a show tune but the show hasn't been written for it yet.")

The red empire of geography classes. "The sun never sets on the British empire and you can't trust it in the dark." Or with the dark peoples. "Because of the Industrial Revolution European countries went in search of markets and raw materials." Another geography (or was it a history) lesson.

Their bloody kings and their bloody queens. Their bloody peers. Their bloody generals. Admirals. Explorers. Livingstone. Hillary. Kitchener. All the bwanas. And all their beaters, porters, sherpas. Who found the source of the Nile. Victoria Falls. The tops of mountains. Their so-called discoveries reek of untruth. How many dark people died so they could misname the physical features in their blasted gazetteer. A statistic we shall never know. Dr. Livingstone, I presume you are here to rape our land and enslave our people.

There are statues of these dead white men all over London.

An interesting fact: The swearword "bloody" is a contraction of "by my lady"—a reference to the Virgin Mary. They do tend to use their ladies. Name ages for them. Places for them. Use them as screens, inspirations, symbols. And many of the ladies comply. While the national martyr Edith Cavell was being executed by the Germans in 1915 in Belgium (called "poor little Belgium" by the allies in the war), the Belgians were engaged in the exploitation of the land and peoples of the Congo.

And will we ever know how many dark peoples were "imported" to fight in whitemen's wars. Probably not. Just as we will never know how many hearts were cut from African people so that the Christian doctor might be a success—i.e., extend a whiteman's life. Our Sister Killjoy observes this from her black-eyed squint.

Dr. Schweitzer—humanitarian, authority on Bach, winner of the Nobel Peace Prize—on the people of Africa: "The Negro is a child, and with children nothing can be done without the use of authority. We must, therefore, so arrange the circumstances of our daily life that my authority can find expression. With regard to Negroes, then, I have coined the formula: 'I am your brother, it is true, but your elder brother.'" (*On the Edge of the Primeval Forest,* 1961)

They like to pretend we didn't fight back. We did: with obeah, poison, revolution. It simply was not enough.

"Colonies. . .these places where 'niggers' are cheap and the earth is rich." (W.E.B. DuBois, "The Souls of White Folk")

A cousin is visiting me from Cal Tech where he is getting a degree in engineering. I am learning about the Italian Renaissance. My cousin is recognizably Black and speaks with an accent. I am not and I do not—unless I am back home, where the "twang" comes upon me. We sit for some time in a bar in his hotel and are not served. A light-skinned Jamaican comes over to our table. He is an older man—a professor at the University of London. "Don't bother with it, you hear. They don't serve us in this bar." A run-of-the-mill incident for all recognizably Black people in this city. But for me it is not.

Henry's eyes fill up, but he refuses to believe our informant. "No, man, the girl is just busy." (The girl is a fifty-year-old white woman, who may just be following orders. But I do not mention this. I have chosen sides.) All I can manage to say is, "Jesus Christ, I hate the fucking English." Henry looks at me. (In the family I am known as the "lady cousin." It has to do with how I look. And the fact that I am twenty-seven and unmarried—and for all they know, unattached. They do not know that I am really the lesbian cousin.) Our informant says—gently, but with a distinct tone of disappointment—"My dear, is that what you're studying at the university?"

You see—the whole business is very complicated.

Henry and I leave without drinks and go to meet some of his white colleagues at a restaurant I know near Covent Garden Opera House. The restaurant caters to theatre types and so I hope there won't be a repeat of the bar scene—at least they know how to pretend. Besides, I tell myself, the owners are Italian *and* gay; they *must* be halfway decent. Henry and his colleagues work for an American company which is paying their way through Cal Tech. They mine bauxite from the hills in the middle of the island and send it to the United States. A turnaround occurs at dinner: Henry joins the whitemen in a sustained mockery of the waiters: their accents and the way they walk. He whispers to me: "Why you want to bring us to a battyman's den, lady?" (*Battyman = faggot* in Jamaican.) I keep quiet.

We put the whitemen in a taxi and Henry walks me to the underground station. He asks me to sleep with him. (It wouldn't be incest. His mother was a maid in the house of an uncle and Henry has not seen her since his birth. He was taken into the family. She was let go.) I say that I can't. I plead exams. I can't say that I don't want to. Because I remember what happened in the bar. But I can't say that I'm a lesbian either— even though I want to believe his alliance with the whitemen at dinner was forced: not really him. He doesn't buy my excuse. "Come on, lady, let's do it. What's the matter, you 'fraid?" I pretend I am back home and start patois to show him somehow I am not afraid, not English, not white. I tell him he's a married man and he tells me he's a ram goat. I take the train to where I am staying and try to forget the whole thing. But I don't. I remember our different skins and our different experiences within them. And I have a hard time realizing that I am angry with Henry. That to him—no use in pretending—a queer is a queer.

1981: I hear on the radio that Bob Marley is dead and I drive over the Mohawk Trail listening to a program of his music and I cry and cry and cry. Someone says: "It wasn't the ganja that killed him, it was poverty and working in a steel foundry when he was young."

I flash back to my childhood and a young man who worked for an aunt I lived with once. He taught me to smoke ganja behind the house. And to peel an orange with the tip of a machete without cutting through the skin—"Love" it was called: a necklace of orange rind the result. I think about him because I heard he had become a Rastaman. And then I think about Rastas.

We are sitting on the porch of an uncle's house in Kingston— the family and I—and a Rastaman comes to the gate. We have guns but they are locked behind a false closet. We have dogs but they are tied up. We are Jamaicans and know that Rastas mean no harm. We let him in and he sits on the side of the porch and shows us his brooms and brushes. We buy some to take back to New York. "Peace, missis."

There were many Rastas in my childhood. Walking the roadside with their goods. Sitting outside their shacks in the mountains. The outsides painted bright—sometimes with words. Gathering at Palisadoes Airport to greet the Conquering Lion of Judah. They were considered figures of fun by most middle-class Jamaicans. Harmless—like Marcus Garvey.

Later: white American hippies trying to create the effect of dred in their straight white hair. The ganja joint held between their straight white teeth. "Man, the grass is good." Hanging out by the Sheraton pool. Light-skinned Jamaicans also dred-locked, also assuming the ganja. Both groups moving to the music but not the words. Harmless. "Peace, brother."

III

My grandmother: "Let us thank God for a fruitful place."
My grandfather: "Let us rescue the perishing world."

This evening on the road in western Massachusetts there are pockets of fog. Then clear spaces. Across from a pond a dog staggers in front of my headlights. I look closer and see that his mouth is foaming. He stumbles to the side of the road—I go to call the police.

I drive back to the house, radio playing "difficult" piano pieces. And I think about how I need to say all this. This is who I am. I am not what you allow me to be. Whatever you decide me to be. In a bookstore in London I show the woman at the counter my book and she stares at me for a minute, then says: "You're a Jamaican." "Yes." "You're not at all like our Jamaicans."

Encountering the void is nothing more nor less than under-standing invisibility. Of being fogbound.

Then: It was never a question of passing. It was a question of hiding. Behind Black and white perceptions of who we were—who they thought we were . Tropics. Plantations. Calypso. Cricket. We were the people with the musical voices and the coronation mugs on our parlor tables. I would be whatever figure these foreign imaginations cared for me to be. It would be so simple to let others fill in for me. So easy to startle them with a flash of anger when their visions got out of hand—but never to sustain the anger for myself.
It could become a life lived within myself. A life cut off. I know who I am but you will never know who I am. I may in fact lose touch with who I am.

I hid from my real sources. But my real sources were also hidden from me.

Now: It is not a question of relinquishing privilege. It is a question of grasping more of myself. I have found that in the real sources are concealed my survival. My speech. My voice. To be colonized is to be rendered insensitive. To have those parts necessary to sustain life numbed. And this is in some cases—in my case—perceived as privilege. The test of a colonized person is to walk through a shantytown in Kingston and not bat an eye. This I cannot do. Because part of me lives there—and as I grasp more of this part I realize what needs to be done with the rest of my life.

Sometimes I used to think we were like the Marranos—the Sephardic Jews forced to pretend they were Christians. The name was given to them by the Christians, and meant "pigs." But once out of Spain and Portugal, they became Jews openly again. Some settled in Jamaica. They knew who the enemy was and acted for their own survival. But they remained Jews always.

We also knew who the enemy was—I remember jokes about the English. Saying they stank. saying they were stingy. that they drank too much and couldn't hold their liquor. that they had bad teeth. were dirty and dishonest. were limey bastards. and horse-faced bitches. We said the men only wanted to sleep with Jamaican women. And that the women made pigs of themselves with Jamaican men.

But of course this was seen by us—the light-skinned middle class—with a double vision. We learned to cherish that part of us that was them—and to deny the part that was not. Believing in some cases that the latter part had ceased to exist.

None of this is as simple as it may sound. We were colorists and we aspired to oppressor status. (Of course, almost any aspiration instilled by western civilization is to oppressor status: success, for example.) Color was the symbol of our potential: color taking in hair "quality," skin tone, freckles, nose-width, eyes. We did not see that color symbolism was a method of keeping us apart: in the society, in the family, between friends. Those of us who were light-skinned, straight-haired, etc., were given to believe that we could actually attain whiteness—or at least those qualities of the colonizer which made him superior. We were convinced of white supremacy. If we failed, we were not really responsible for our failures: we had all the advantages—but it was that one persistent drop of blood, that single rogue gene that made us unable to con-ceptualize abstract ideas, made us love darkness rather than despise it, which was to be blamed for our failure. Our dark part had taken over: an inherited imbalance in which the doom of the creole was sealed.

I am trying to write this as clearly as possible, but as I write I realize that what I say may sound fabulous, or even mythic. It is. It is insane.

Under this system of colorism—the system which prevailed in my childhood in Jamaica, and which has carried over to the present—rarely will dark and light people co-mingle. Rarely will they achieve between themselves an intimacy informed with identity. (I should say here that I am using the categories light and dark both literally and symbolically. There are dark Jamaicans who have achieved lightness and the "advantages" which go with it by their successful pursuit of oppressor status.)

Under this system light and dark people will meet in those ways in which the light-skinned person imitates the oppressor. But imitation goes only so far: the light-skinned person becomes an oppressor in fact. He/she will have a dark chauffeur, a dark nanny, a dark maid, and a dark gardener. These employees will be paid badly. Because of the slave past, because of their dark skin, the servants of the middle class have been used according to the traditions of the slavocracy. They are not seen as workers for their own sake, but for the sake of the family who has employed them. It was not until Michael Manley became prime minister that a minimum wage for houseworkers was enacted—and the indignation of the middle class was profound.

During Manley's leadership the middle class began to abandon the island in droves. Toronto. Miami. New York. Leaving their houses and businesses behind and sewing cash into the tops of suitcases. Today—with a new regime—they are returning:

"Come back to the way things used to be" the tourist advertise-
ment on American t.v. says. "Make it Jamaica again. Make it
your own."

But let me return to the situation of houseservants as I
remember it: They will be paid badly, but they will be "given"
room and board. However, the key to the larder will be kept by
the mistress in her dresser drawer. They will spend Christmas
with the family of their employers and be given a length of
English wool for trousers or a few yards of cotton for dresses.
They will see their children on their days off: their extended
family will care for the children the rest of the time. When the
employers visit their relations in the country, the servants may
be asked along—oftentimes the servants of the middle class
come from the same part of the countryside their employers
have come from. But they will be expected to work while they
are there. Back in town, there are parts of the house they are
allowed to move freely around; other parts they are not
allowed to enter. When the family watches the t.v. the servant
is allowed to watch also, but only while standing in a doorway.
The servant may have a radio in his/her room, also a dresser
and a cot. Perhaps a mirror. There will usually be one ceiling
light. And one small square louvered window.

A true story: One middle-class Jamaican woman ordered a
Persian rug from Harrod's in London. The day it arrived so did
her new maid. She was going downtown to have her hair
touched up, and told the maid to vacuum the rug. She told the
maid she would find the vacuum cleaner in the same shed as
the power mower. And when she returned she found that the
fine nap of her new rug had been removed.

The reaction of the mistress was to tell her friends that the
"girl" was backward. She did not fire her until she found that
the maid had scrubbed the teflon from her new set of pots,
saying she thought they were coated with "nastiness."

The houseworker/mistress relationship in which one Black woman is the oppressor of another Black woman is a cornerstone of the experience of many Jamaican women.

I remember another true story: In a middle-class family's home one Christmas, a relation was visiting from New York. This woman had brought gifts for everybody, including the housemaid. The maid had been released from a mental institution recently, where they had "treated" her for depression. This visiting light-skinned woman had brought the dark woman a bright red rayon blouse and presented it to her in the garden one afternoon, while the family was having tea. The maid thanked her softly, and the other woman moved toward her as if to embrace her. Then she stopped, her face suddenly covered with tears, and ran into the house, saying, "My God, I can't, I can't."

We are women who come from a place almost incredible in its beauty. It is a beauty which can mask a great deal and which has been used in that way. But that the beauty is there is a fact. I remember what I thought the freedom of my childhood, in which the fruitful place was something I took for granted. Just as I took for granted Zoe's appearance every morning on my school vacations—in the sense that I knew she would be there. That she would always be the one to visit me. The perishing world of my grandfather's graces at the table, if I ever seriously thought about it, was somewhere else.

Our souls were affected by the beauty of Jamaica, as much as they were affected by our fears of darkness.

There is no ending to this piece of writing. There is no way to end it. As I read back over it, I see that we/they/I may become confused in the mind of the reader: but these pronouns have always co-existed in my mind. The Rastas talk of the "I and I"—a pronoun in which they combine themselves with Jah. Jah is a contraction of Jahweh and Jehova, but to me always sounds like the beginning of Jamaica. I and Jamaica is who I am. No matter how far I travel—how deep the ambivalence I feel about ever returning. And Jamaica is a place in which we/they/I connect and disconnect—change place.

Love in the Third World

The Land of Look Behind

On the edge of each canefield or "piece" was a watch house, a tiny structure with one entry. These were used for the babies of nursing slaves who worked in the fields. An older woman was in charge of the infants and the mothers came there for feeding time.

tourist brochure of the Whim Great House

A tiny structure with one entry
walls guttered with mortar
molasses   coral   sand
hold the whole thing fast.

One hundred years later
the cut limestone
sunned and salted
looks like new.

And feels like? And feels like?
I don't know.
Describe it.
Sad? Lost? Angry?
Let me get my bearings.

Outside
A tamarind tree with a dead nest in the first crotch
Dense mud construction.
Immense. The inhabitants long gone.
Hard brown pods crack underfoot
The soursweet flesh is dried.
Inedible.

Inside
One thin bench faces a blank wall.
No message from the watchwomen here.
No HELP ME carved in the mortar or the stone.
Try to capture the range—

What did their voices sound like?
What tongues? What words for day and night?
Hunger? Milk?
What songs devised to ease them?

Was there time to speak? To sing?
To the riverain goddesses
The mermaids bringing secrets
To bring down Shàngó's wrath.

No fatting-houses here.
Nowhere to learn the secrets
except through some new code
in spaces they will never own.

How many voices? How many drops of milk?
How many gums daubed with rum to soothe the teething
or bring on sleep?

Shàngó is the Yoruban god of thunder and lightning and vengeance.

How many breasts bore scars?
Not the sacred markings of the Carib—
but the mundane mark of the beast.

How many dropped in the field?
How many bare footfalls across the sand floor?
How many were buried?
I leave through the opening and take myself home.

Make It Your Own

"But it's so beautiful—more than I expected
but too sad
and too poor. How can you stand to be so poor?"

He skips to the sands—"so white"—and the sea
"at least five shades of blue."

"And I understand a reef keeps the sharks from the beaches.
That's lucky."
Only for you, massa.

The reef is coral.
Foot-tearing white coral.
White coral with sanded crevices.
Fat brain coral.
From here the reef seems smoothed by salt. As though you
could walk barefooted across the waves. Not so.

Nobody—as far as I know—planned it. It's just that their hotels
were built with an eye to the whiteness of the sands. Native
beaches are stony black—volcanic. With underwater sinkholes
and no reef. I have seen the gray-skin sails circling, the sun
lighting their passage through the waves.

Shall I tell him that we chose a pale child to come along
because sharks are startled by white skin and more likely to
attack him? Or about the woman who walked from the sea on
one leg, never knowing the other was gone? Or the shark
caught with a seaman's papers in his gullet?

The sea is something we live with. It is around us. Beneath us
too.

The wrecks of history—shall I tell him about those? The account books, their ink running into the bottom of the sea. The rusted iron links. The sea hides these from his view. And ours too. Hides the silent toothed barracuda who can negotiate any reef. And the flat languid ray.

Shall I tell him about the afternoon a cousin and I spent in a mangrove swamp picking oysters from the trunks of the trees? Up to our knees in salt water. How we fled when we spotted the flick of an alligator's tail a few yards away. My cousin dropped his cutlass and I fell forward, getting a fine wound on my thigh and leaving blood in the water.

No. I won't say anything.

". . .and your food is so interesting.
I didn't know people ate goats. Or turtle either.
What does turtle taste like?"

Turtle.

"And the children. Such beautiful smiles. They seem so happy. Where *do* they get their teeth?"

From the coarse wood of the cane—rubbing them white, but leaving a residue of sugar. When he returns—as he will—will he notice the gaps in teenage mouths? Or just call them unsmiling, sullen?

"No one at my hotel seemed belligerent. Or angry. I had been warned about you. That Jamaicans are arrogant. Probably because you derive in part from the Carib tribe. Didn't they devour their enemies?"

Yes. Just not enough of them.

"But you are fond of your sex and rum, aren't you?"

Wouldn't you be? But then you are a manager of the world and need to keep your wits about you. Else we might steal the world right under your eyes. No fear.

"You drove me in a taxi and took me straight to where I wanted to go. Didn't take advantage. But you do drive fast. Careless. And you whip around those drays. Why do you let them clutter up the road? Surely you people have heard of pick-ups? And why do you keep to the left? The English influence, I guess."

It is time to respond.

"Well, your destination was the Sheraton. From Palisadoes Airport that is about ten miles. You pass by the National Stadium where we held Bob Marley's funeral and the children danced in mourning white. That is about five miles from your hotel.

"Yes, children can dance at funerals. It's meant to ease their pain. No, they don't wear white to reflect the sun; they wear it to signify death.

"You say we drove you—and how many of us were driving, may I ask?—please don't answer. You say we drove you via Mona. What you saw wasn't a penitentiary. No, not a factory. Did you not see the sign? Hardly a zoo. That was our university. Yes, we have a university. And a medical school. No, not for Americans; for us. Perhaps we needed to show you something besides the hotels. Don't ask me why. Our mistake. We took you in the opposite direction than where you wanted to go. About twenty miles. I don't know exactly. But we measure our distances in palm trees here, so please forgive us any inaccuracy."

He asks—in all seriousness—how one measures distances in palm trees.

"The distance between two royal palms—the royal palms are the ones that stand straight and do not bear coconut—is equivalent to the first two furlongs in a horserace when, and only then, the horses run counterclockwise. Unless of course there is a dwarf coconut in between. Then you must find the circumference of the two royal palms flanking the dwarf divided by seven. It is an African system of measurement."

All puzzlement fades. He nods slowly. The word *African* has made the trick sensible to him.

"Do you have many connections with Africa?"

"We have diplomatic relations with the African nations. Of course we do not recognize the government of South Africa, as we once did under colonialism, although that may change under Mr. Seaga."

"But surely there is nothing to be gained by not speaking."

"I beg your pardon?"

"Surely you have heard of constructive engagement?"

"Yes."

"You may think that is going too far, but it seems to me you can't turn your back on people. I mean, I think the whites are simply frightened, surrounded by that hostile black mass."

"Are you frightened?"

"I don't get your meaning."

"I wish you were. I wish sometimes we had it in our power to terrify you. And that your terror would come from a righteous place, and not the usual source of your fear—whatever image you have projected onto us. I wish you were sweating about our power. I wish your heart would burst from your chest and your aorta flood your extremities with blood. And that this blood seeped from your pores and blinded you. I wish we could destroy you without harming ourselves."

"I had no idea you felt that way. . . . Anyhow, I wasn't speaking about that kind of relationship with Africa. I meant do you people reminisce about your African connection. Your point of origin."

"I don't think reminisce is the proper word."

"Maybe not. But you seem to have gotten so hostile—all of a sudden."

"Not at all."

"I mean, we do bring our money here. We put you on the map."

"So you did."

The Laughing Mulatto (Formerly a Statue) Speaks

Now I have seen so many of you up close—and turn back and away from all but a few. You cannot accommodate my rage. You who come to eye me in the town square.

Periwinkles and foxgloves and even pungent marigolds, plain-jane flowers, give me comfort. The earth filled with worms after the spring thaw. The cutworms who wait curled tight to gorge themselves by night on the silvered stalks of the cabbages. Stunted raintree. Bats gliding from the barn at seven each summer evening. Heavy-headed sunflowers feeding the gros-beaks and sparrows and jays. Woodpeckers drawing grubs from the catalpa. Mother skunk rummaging among empty shells and stripped bones to feed her babies in the wet earth cellar; the flash of my light only makes her more determined. These beings and these acts deepen my life in ways so few of you are able.

I love so few of you whose skin rejects light. I did not want it this way.

I am writing the story of my life as a statue. But no kiss set me free to speak.

I wish they had carved me from the onyx of Elizabeth Catlett. Or molded me from the dark clay of Augusta Savage. Or cut me from mahogany or cast me in bronze. I wish I were dark plaster like Meta Warrick Fuller's *Talking Skull*. But I appear more as Edmonia Lewis's *Hagar*—wringing her hands in the wilder-ness—white marble figure of no homeland—her striations caught within.

I remember three sisters: three women in particular. They left flowers for me and notes and exacted promises that I would never tell. Would not crack the surface—the smooth unblemished surface that was me.

Come back now sisters. Now I can speak. But they are gone never to come back.

I am talking about three real women. One dead. Two living. Who chose to live as ghosts. And whom I understand. And whom I have tried to love.

From a letter to Capt. P.B.S. Pinchback (the grandfather of Jean Toomer) from his sister Addie Saffold:

Pink I feel sorry for your sad situation yet at the same time I feel angry at you. . .angry to see you classing yourself among the despised race. . . . In all the wide world there is no safety for the Negro but Pink *we* are *not* Negroes. I consider myself the equal of any in the world. . . .

Girl, what made you confuse your priorities so?
Why do I care what you said a hundred years ago?
Because you are lost to me, and I to you.
We are—because of who we are—unsafe.
And no amount of nonsense will protect you.

Within the Veil

Color ain't no faucet
You can't turn it off and on
I say, color ain't no faucet
You can't turn it off and on
Tell the world who you are
Or you might as well be gone.

Now, the whiteman makes the rules
But we got to learn to turn them down
Yes, baby, the whiteman makes the rules
But we got to learn to turn them down
Can't abide this shit no longer
We got to swing the thing around.

You can pass in many ways, mama
This is one thing that I know
I say, you can pass in many ways, mama
This is one thing that I know
Unless you quit your passing, honey
You only gonna come to woe.

Oh, we can call them ofay
By that we mean the foe
Yes, sisters, we can call them ofay
By that we mean the foe
But that's only half the battle
You lie if you tell me you don't know.

Now Zora was a genius
But there were some did call her fool
I say, Zora was a genius
But there were some did call her fool
Now, you consider mules and men
And how many times she broke the whiteman's rule.

Some of us come from islands
And some of us born in the U.S.A.
Some of us come from islands
And some of us born in the U.S.A.
There are those of us who marry
And others who will always be gay.

No two people are the same
It's what gives life a thrilling twist
No two people are the same, children
That's what gives life a thrilling twist
How dare anyone object
Tell me I had better not exist.

Some of us use the hot comb
And some of us have natural hair
Yes, sisters, some of us use the hot comb
And some of us have natural hair
You should ponder Madame C. J. Walker
Before you suck your teeth and stare.

Sister Lorraine talked revolution
Talked of "the beauty of things Black"
Yes, Lorraine talked revolution, baby
Talked of "the beauty of things Black"
And then she was killed by cancer
Just like a well-aimed shot in her strong brown back.

Your best friend's a bulldagger
That is very plain to see
I say, your best friend's a bulldagger
That is very plain to see
Now that you been told it
Can you tell them you love me?

We got to love each other
That is what is known as the bottom line
I say, we got to love each other
That is what they call the bottom line
Can't say to each other
To hell with you, this piece of the world is mine.

Some of us part Indian
And some of us part white
Yes, sisters, some of us part Indian
And some of us part white
But we still will call you sisters
Even if you judge our skin too light.

Gold chains are love-symbols
You tell me where they are found
Yes, gold chains are love-symbols
You tell me where gold is found
There are deep mines in South Africa
Where our brothers sweat their lives underground.

God loves the babies in Soweto
And the babies in Harlem too
I say, God loves the babies in Soweto
And the babies in Harlem too
But his love alone can't save them
We got to figure what we can do.

If we say Third World Revolution
The white folks say World War III
If we say Third World Revolution, baby
The white folks say World War III
Seems they imagine Armageddon
Is prettier than if we be free.

I got brothers and sisters in prison
All across the U.S.A.
Yes, I got brothers and sisters in prison
All across the U.S.A.
Some folks broke the rules
Others just been put away.

Elijah Pate was gunned down
Shot five times by the Boston cops
Yes, Brother Elijah was gunned down
Shot five times by the Boston cops
And the d.a. won't bring charges
Says Elijah gunned his car and wouldn't stop.

They want us in their factories
And they want us in their homes
I say, they want us in their factories
and they want us in their homes
They'll take some for their armed forces
And some more for their astrodomes.

They see our brothers as monsters
Or as harmless smart-assed little boys
They judge our brothers to be monsters
Want to keep them harmless little boys
Let just one speak his piece
And watch the guns replace the toys.

Don't overstep your boundaries
Act like you have a little sense
No, don't overstep your boundaries, girl
Act like you have a little sense
Was the lesson my mama taught me
To live surrounded by a whiteman's fence.

It's all about survival
And about how to get by
Yes, it's all about survival
And about how to get by
But we got to do it better
Else we might as well lay down and die.

Heartache

Heartbroken.

> Josh Gibson
> Jackie Robinson
> Elston Howard
> Arthur Ashe

Broken-hearted.

> Jim Thorpe (Bright Path)

> "Some say Josh Gibson died of a brain hemorrhage. I
> say he died of a broken heart."

> Ted Page, ballplayer in the Negro leagues

Our brothers die every minute—so it seems.
Dead in the quiet of their dreams
or when the dreams run out
or running from the man
or hanging from a limb
or of too much stuff
or from the shots of some white cop
or alone in SRO's
or when the rage turns in
or from trying to overcome.

The baseball diamond—cut in the hard grass heart of America—
held something. Free and gracious movement. Moving even as
the faceless shot their mouths off—the word that hurt present
even in praise. Mays flying. Gibson fireballing. Brock stealing
home.

When the movement slows it is something else again.

A story in a newspaper about a Black football player from Indiana—cut from the team. A young Black man with a wife and a three-week-old daughter. A young Black man who was—according to all interviewed—gentle and hardworking and loving and honest and beautiful and who was studying for his college degree even though his athletic scholarship had been cancelled. I read how he had been killed by some white cops who shot him five times. He had no weapon. They claimed he was acting "strange" and they were frightened. So they shot him. He had no history of behaving "strange." He found himself downtown and turned around and five white cops with five guns drawn surrounded him. Maybe he asked to be left alone. Asked these frightening men to leave him alone. He did not want to die. Realizing what would happen despite his unarmed state what were his thoughts?

And then his story—as such histories always do—disappeared. But it re-emerges in other deaths from day to day and week to week. While the killers walk.

I say this and I leave you with three names: Juanita Thomas. Bernadette Powell. Roxanne Gay.

Jaffrey Center, New Hampshire

A white/white graveyard is filled with dead babies—weeping willows and urns carved into slate. The same stonecarver's name repeats and repeats. Little childish fingers point upward. Dead women. Dead men. Civil War dead. Revolutionary dead. The history of a village.

It is May. There are blackflies who eat my thighs through my jeans. And one rapid little chipmunk who springs from headstone to headstone. Heart's ease and violets bloom underfoot.

But the white/white graveyard is not so white
On a hill—side by side—off from the others

Sacred to the memory	Sacred to the memory
of Amos Fortune, who	of Violate, by sale the slave
was born free in Africa,	of Amos Fortune,
a slave in America,	by marriage his wife,
he purchased liberty,	by her fidelity his friend
professed Christianity,	and solace,
lived reputably, and	she died his widow.
died hopefully.	
November 17, 1801	September 13, 1802
AET. 91	AET. 73

Found poems they call discoveries like these. The flies swarm around me as I try to rub the stones—I light a cigarette and see my grandmother's face. I am being disrespectful—but it is the only way to keep the bugs at bay. But the inscriptions are too smoothed by time and only a blur is transferred to my white butcher paper.

The Crazy Teepee

I am attracted to places where things are buried.

Dear Beth, dear friend,

Yesterday I felt depressed. So I did what any sane American would do: rented a nice big car from your city—silver Reliant with red leatherette seats.

I blasted the fm radio on a golden oldies station and went fast—past the trailers and farms on the backroads, most in need of repair. Listened—and sang along. Then I felt better. Of course I would have felt even better if Bessie had been singing "Taint Nobody's Business If I Do" or if Billie had called on "huggable, lovable Emily Brown/ Miss Brown to you." But the best I could do was John Lennon and Peggy Lee. "The Music of Your Life" the program was called—smile.

I took my rented car on an expedition: THE CRAZY TEEPEE. You would have loved the crazy teepee at the side of route 191.
36 rooms of "used goods" they explain. 36 rooms of bits and
       pieces.
Inside the teepee—around 36 corners and through 36
       corridors—
are broken commodes
bins of patchouli and musk and love potions
vials and votive candles
a wedgwood plate of plastic—the same pattern we had when I
was a kid. A crockery prize at the A&P. I tried—then as now—
to transport myself across the bridge and through the
cypresses.
abandoned Chinese restaurant tea-sets
an enormous barrel of crutches.

Poor white people abound in the 36 rooms.
They know I am not serious. I have no children with me. I pass my hands over objects in an abstracted way. If the pattern or feel takes me back I smile—extending the time I touch. If not, I move on. It seems I have no need.

Except a need for the past?

A dancing man startles me. His wooden platform is cracked down the middle—the stick to hold him straight is missing. But his legs dangle intact. My father comes back.

A young woman with a tiny baby rummages systematically through the old clothes stuffed on racks in no order of size or type. Boy Scout uniforms hang beside old prom dresses. Decorated VFW gear is partly hidden by housedresses. The woman turns back item after item and her baby dozes at her shoulder.

I can come from having my nipples sucked. And this gives me pleasure but also makes me feel unreal. As if I have exchanged one purpose for another—unjustified.

Dust rises
from lanterns
cracked ball jars
bowling balls
bottles—one so old the glass has gone translucent. Like a puddle of gasoline it makes purple and green rainbows.

Hundreds of books. The same ones we're used to seeing in secondhand bazaars. Church basements. Tag sales.
Strange Fruit—which always seems to be everywhere. How many people must have read it? Here for 40¢. For once I pass it by.
Laura Z. Hobson's *Gentlemen's Agreement*

Betty Smith's *A Tree Grows in Brooklyn*
Fannie Hurst's *Imitation of Life*
Saturday afternoon reading from a long time ago.

Stacks of *Penthouse* bring me back to where I am. A shapeless owl-eyed man riffles through. I leave the bookroom because it is dimly lit and too far from the exit and his enthusiasm unnerves me.

There are a lot of dirty tricks in the crazy teepee
whoopee cushions
bugs in ice cubes
fake vomit.

Next to the room of broken appliances and board-games
missing markers   cordless lamps   and old 45s
is the room which made me dream of you last night.
The room which gave the place its name. The Indian room—
filled with phony tomahawks and tom-toms and totems. Mass-production versions of pottery and carving. Gimmicks of holy images. Velvet reproductions of *The End of the Trail*. You know the stuff. All the regalia and warclubs and arrows scaled down to what white America calls "child-sized." Rubberized and harmless and stamped *created by the Cherokee Nation*.

I should have expected it to be the way it was. The dream I had was just as obvious and bold: we went through the crazy teepee and smashed everything—that simple. We didn't explain.

Artificial Skin

Slip me some artificial skin, Daddy
Doctor Do-Wrong, won't you do right by me
elastic and plastic
a dash of color, please

Beg pardon? Your research hasn't gone that far? You say you
don't intend to go that far?

What you say?
Therapeutic and not cosmetic, you say?
But, man, color *is* therapeutic—i.e., I need it for my well-being.

Just think—you could call it the Melanin Project. Like a sci-fi
space-age fantasy. Make a t.v. mini-series. Call it Color Wars.
The Return of Nefertiti. Cosmetic Cosmos. Forbidden Pigment.

Big Bucks—you know, like you made from *King Kong*. And all
those *Planets of the Apes*. Now weren't *they* thinly disguised.

"Melanin to earth. . .Melanin to earth. . ."
"Earth responding: Maybe you people should orbit a little
while longer."

(Upon reading about the development of artificial skin and
seeing a few samples on t.v.)

Constructive Engagement

with: the sisters and brothers on the sun-blasted dried-out bantustans/ the goldminers/ the white-baby minders/ the diamond miners/ the forced laborers/ the Ford auto workers/ the house workers/ the urban dwellers/ the urban workers/ the coloreds/ the hungry ones/ the old ones/ the prisoners/ the ones whose children are dead/ the ones whose children are still alive/ the schoolchildren/ the law-breakers/ the ones who have no work/ the ones who have been reclassified/ the pass-carriers/ the ones whose passes have been voided/ the white-sewer tenders/ the ones who wear the Black Sash/ the lovers.

with: Mamphela Ramphele/ Albertina Sisulu/ Albert Luthuli/ Ruth First/ Winnie Mandela/ Helen Suzman/ Helen Joseph/ Steve Biko/ Nelson Mandela—a few names I got from reading the papers.

I read the papers every day. I see a picture of a Black girlchild in a courtroom as she describes in her own words where her friend, a seven-year-old boychild, was standing with his bike (at the curb) when a car driven by a white male ran him down and dragged him a hundred feet. Her friend was crushed and she saw all this. The young white male (described as "neatly dressed" by the paper) is on trial for her friend's murder. When I look at the face of this little girl, framed with braided hair and ribbon bows, and when I read her testimony, I think about her. I ask questions. Did anything stop in her when she saw her friend die? Does she dream about that afternoon? Is she afraid? Does she feel guilty for not saving him? Did she think she could save him? Does she understand what happened? Are there people who will protect her from this knowledge? Does she understand her own courage—for that *is* what it is—in standing up, school-dress, hair braided, in a white court before a white judge and a white jury and a white defendant and his white friends and white family who claim it was only an accident while she is questioned by a white d.a. and a white defense lawyer and points her slender brown finger to the place on the three-dimensional model of that afternoon where she insists her friend stood—and no amount of tricky questioning can shake her. Does she shake inside? Does she know that she is a loving friend? Does she think about enemies? That her enemy has shown his face to her? Can she realize that there are people who will hate her without ever meeting her? What will happen in her life?

Tell me if I saw what I thought I saw. Tell me if you will whether this happened in New York or Pretoria, L. A. or Johannesburg.

Don't ever tell me that South Africa makes America better by comparison.

Battle Royal

(Thoughts on the invasion of Grenada and Carriacou)

1st rule for invaders: learn to pronounce the names of places you invade.

2nd rule for invaders: give the children what they want—that is, offer them Hershey bars and Wrigley's gum and then shoot them with your camera when they thank you.

3rd rule for invaders: watch out for old ladies who work roots. They may cost you your manhood. Shoot any old lady with a burlap sack over her back. No one will know.

4th rule for invaders: look out for beautiful women. They may be booby-trapped   armed   have the clap. Shoot them on sight.

5th rule for invaders: these people are uncivilized. Monkey-chasers. Shoot them if they seem hostile. Laugh at them if they seem friendly; if they turn hostile, shoot them.

6th rule for invaders: bomb any large building—it may be a cache of ammo. Bomb any mental hospital—it may hold revolutionaries. Bomb any small shack—it may hold an underground tunnel to the rest of the Third World.

7th rule for invaders: these people are your enemy. Take my word for it. Do not love them.

Love in the Third World

exists.

Love in the Third World can be just as powerful/complicated/
multileveled/varied/long-standing
as in the First or Second Worlds—maybe more so.
as on the moons of Jupiter
or through the dusty rings of Saturn—maybe more so.
in the blood-red canals of Mars
the clouded circumference of Venus
the tumultuous speck of hot Mercury—maybe more so.
as much as on the dangerous surface of Uranus
through the wild orbit of Neptune
or on distant dependable Pluto—maybe more so.

A Jamaican woman visits home and returns with a photograph.
Two women live together in a structure made of packing crates
behind the Kingston Parish Church. She met one of them on a
bus and was invited to dinner. The women arrange the
contents of their crates for company and build a fire where
they make yam and banana and salted codfish. Their King
James sits on an upended Ovaltine box—a prize from some-
one's Sunday School. The women cover another box with a
piece of crocus sack and serve their meal on flattened milk tins
and cracked enamel utensils cleaned under the city standpipe
nearby. At least, the photographer says, they have each other.

Yes. But the simple and final and flat question is why—on this
Black island-nation, our motto being "out of many, one
people"—are two Black women living as they must. And it
does not really matter whether their crates are labeled
Westinghouse or General Electric or Purveyors to Her Majesty
the Queen. Please don't tell me it's very complicated or that

there will always be people like these who choose to live on city streets. Don't tell me that if it hadn't been for the shanties Bob Marley would never have existed. Don't tell me the climate causes such distress, but if we are warm we can't be truly miserable. Or that the trees bear for everyone and there are windfalls to be gathered if only our people weren't so lazy.

I know the price of cooking oil and rice.
I know the price of Blue Mountain coffee and Canadian saltfish.
I have a sense of the depth of our self-hatred.
I speak from a remove of time and space—I have tried to hold your shape and history within me. I keep track of you through advertisements and photographs. Through *The Harder They Come* and "Natty Dread." By entering the patty shops in Bedford-Stuyvesant. By watching a group of applepickers stroll through a Massachusetts hilltown. Through the shots of graffitti on the walls of Tivoli Gardens. My homeland. My people.

I wonder if I will ever return—I light a cigarette to trap the fear of what returning would mean. And this is something I will admit only to you. I am afraid my place is at your side. I am afraid my place is in the hills. This is a killing ambivalence. I bear in mind that you with all your cruelties are the source of me, and like even the most angry mother draw me back.

A Pilgrimage, a History Lesson, Two Satires, and a Vision

A Visit to the Secret Annex

> What kinds of times are these, when
> A talk about trees is almost a crime
> Because it implies a silence about so many
> horrors?
>
> Bertolt Brecht, "For Those Born Later"

I was born later
not into this world.
The trees were not the same
The horrors not exact—but similar

I walk along the *Prinsengracht*—a late-spring afternoon
a visitor—cooled by the air from the canals.

I sight my destination—pass it by
Return on the heels of a group of schoolchildren.

The stairs stretch up
into perpendicular flights
I begin my climb.

I had not expected my feelings to be so. . .What?
(Then why did I turn around?)

Cold sweat pours out of my head and through the cloth of my burgundy shirt. The back of my shirt sticks flat. I can feel it darkening.

(By now I have learned to fight
pretending I am not touched.)

Here in these narrow, empty rooms
(Why do I say "empty"? The place is filled with other people—
silent people reading the legends and walking back and forth—
past the ornamental toilet—baroque, green scrolls curl around
two birds with tails entwined on the bowl. Delft? I wonder.)

Here in these rooms alone I am terrified of tears (and what follows? shame? embarrassment?) and feel an onslaught coming if I give in.

I lock my eyes. Sweat pours out instead   tidal   salt.
Redirected by my bitten lips and tongue from the pinpoints at the corners of my eyes to the entire surface of my body. My skin.

Yes, my girl. I say this to myself. (Because part of me is a girl and part of me is a woman speaking to her.) Here is the heroine you once had and wondered about.

The girl you loved.

I meet her suspended in this place. At thirteen, fourteen, fifteen. At four or so a Montessori student. A baby held by an elegant mother.

Would I have changed places
were that the only choice?

I glance at the two walls where she fixed her pinups.
Norma Shearer, Deanna Durbin, Ginger Rogers—lips reddened
wildly from the rotogravure.
There are pictures of the "little princesses"—Elizabeth and
Margaret Rose
Another picture showing roses. In the foreground of a country
house. Her dream house? Didn't we all have dream houses?

The *Westerkerk* next-door strikes four. A window is open wide
onto a huge flowering chestnut in the garden of the church.

I turn to the tree. Breathe in its blossoms. Watch its fat leaves
move against a bright-blue sky.

I do not know how to calculate the ages of trees. (I have
studied closely how to calculate the ages of churches.)

I remember the childhood advice about the rings in a tree's
insides. But I can't slice the tree open. Just to tell if it's forty or
so.

I hold a conversation with myself about trees.
To see if she might have had a living tree as a companion—
even a tree in a churchyard—instead of one cut from colored
paper.

Still, she would have only sensed the tree, had the tree been
there.

Still, she might have listened for the hard drop of the fruit in fall,
while her father tracked the advance of the allies on his little
map. Imagined gathering the chestnuts and roasting them at
the side of a canal busy with barges and small family boats.

But she would never have seen her tree—the windows of the hiding place were always shaded, covered with paper or painted blue.
To keep their existences secret   safe.

Had she cracked the pane to peek as her tree flowered, or shed its fruit or leaves, she would have been killed.
Sooner.

Ah. . .the congregations of the *Westerkerk*, not knowing a group of Jews hovered above them, above their chestnut tree.
Thinking they were *Judenrein*.

Europe Becomes Blacker

The world is white no longer, and it will never be white
again.

James Baldwin, *Notes of a Native Son*

Europe becomes Blacker
but it was always dark, you know.
And I'm not talking about Dumas, *père*
or *fils*, for that matter
whose blood went back
to Africa by way of Haiti.
Or Pushkin, whose grandpa started as a slave
named Hannibal and became a military engineer
under Peter the Great
And while we're on the subject: What about the Black General
Hannibal and all his Black troops in the Alps—
did they linger?

Some of the blood in Europe runs right
back to Africa
And I don't mean Josephine Baker's adopted brood in Périgord
alone.
I mean the Moors—you know, European Black folks
I mean slaves—
captured on the trails blazed by whites in mad pursuit
of Blackness (which they always seem to be—one way or
        another)
and Black power—which they used
to run sugar plantations on Cyprus—and that's just one
        example.

And now more colored folks are coming home to roost
And I'm not talking about Bricktop's *bôite*
Mabel Mercer—who swore she was Welsh

or nightspots like *Le Joyeux Nègre*
Those days are gone.

I'm talking about the offspring of Zulus and Maroons
Algerian and Jamaican and Ghanaian factory-workers
Tuareg and Pakistani and Ibo bus-conductors
Surinamese and Moluccan and Kikuyu dish-washers
Trinidadian and Antillean and Cruzan farm-workers
Vietnamese and Javanese and Taiwanese laborers
Some hidden for years in state barracks so outsiders
and insiders will not suspect the extent of the Blackness
of Europe
(and in the hope—great and white—that Blackness won't seep
out—though, as we know, it's far more likely that whiteness
will seep in
Remember the quarters?)
Which brings me to the children of mixture—
die Mischlingen
bambini de sangue misto
the crossover babies.
There are millions of us. We number in the millions.

Europe has not been *Schwärzenrein*
for a long time now.
And I don't just mean the Black cardinal
entombed in the Vatican during the *Cinquecento*
Or Shirley Bassey singing *Goldfinger*
Or Cleo Laine.

All those gypsies shoveled into ovens
Now they were dark people too.

A Visit from Mr. Botha

I

(In the summer of 1984, President Botha of the Republic
of South Africa visits whitish Europe.)

Perhaps, he thinks, they could use some advice
Before the Black folks are all over them
like white on rice.

Advice on how to limit colored birth
And stop these people moving across the earth
as if they owned it.

First things first:
Fertility must be diminished
And then this dangerous influx can be finished
once and for all.
But just enough to ensure a manageable workforce
A delicate balance can be obtained by force
alone.

Slice her tubes, then scrape the woman's walls—
eliminate the baby and its caul.
Insert a shield—she cannot realize
Before her eyes, she has been neutralized.

Now, as to the ones amongst you:

Separate them! That has always been our answer,
he declares over tea with Mrs. Thatcher.
Keep families apart, dear lady, hire watchmen
Teach your best bobbies to be expert gunmen
Send them flying into crowds with armored lorries
That should begin to put aside your worries.

Policemen can be trained for tasks like this
Get some dark ones, Scotland Yard will make you lists
of like prospects, ones who will be sucked
into thinking, by their loyalty, they're now in luck.
Pathetic fallacy, damn fools, but we can use it.
Give them false power, allow them to abuse it.
Turn them one against the other,
that's the ticket,
They'll turn from their brothers
and brutalize the pickets.
As to women and children, that can be a sticky wicket.

World sympathy, you know, pictures of wounded kiddies
can be harmful to our cause, among the liberal ladies
and some men too, although we're a bit more realistic
knowing shopping bags can hold explosives made of plastic.
Remember Algeria? Who is innocent in this battle?
Not the schoolchild, not the baby with its rattle
which might be aimed at a guardsman's noble head
You may laugh, but they wish we all were dead.

But not too much force against the women and children
Illness will do the job; encourage malnutrition.
Let nature take its course, that's very plain, sir
(Excuse me, madam)
One day, who knows, they all may die of cancer.

Mrs. T thinks Mr. B's a sensible gent
She thanks him as he heads for the Continent.

The leaders of several other whitish states
Tell Mr. Botha help may come too late.
They're all around us, want to claim their rights
as citizens—we must work day and night
to stop them; it will be a dreadful pity
if they take over every Christian city
if they overrun our parks and universities
and in museums put their dark obscenities
called *art*.
The stench of their food can actually stop the breath
and hangs over us, like a silent sign of death
Forgive me if I sound a little queer
but I prefer the smell of Camembert
to curry.
Where do we put them? You are large; we're small
We don't have landroom to secrete them all
We can't build more enclosures; there's not time
and some of our white citizens will call crime
One speaks alone: This will take all our wits
Too bad, he muses, there's no more Auschwitz
Out of order, sir! That is too austere
We need right now only to remove our fear
of them taking over; limit their movement, I say
So we know their whereabouts every hour, every day
No, no, no—there's conflict among the whole damn lot
of leaders—who can't agree on what and what's not
permissible.

Mr. B is growing weary of this bunch
His tummy growls; it's nearly time for lunch.
If desperate call in soldiers; let them do it all
Pardon me, I need to make a call
To a leading churchman, he's meeting now with Margaret
who will see if he agrees on our target
and has a blessing for the execution of our plan
He is a realistic, if devoutly silly, man.

Yes, churchmen are quite helpful to the cause
They help both pass and abrogate the laws.
In South Africa we have a firm alliance
We took the inexact and made it science.
Using the Bible, conjuring arguments and tricks
We've figured how hatred can be holy and exist
successfully.

We face an age-old problem, my dear friends
Of how to use their labor but obstruct their ends
which means only revolution, that Black farce
we've seen them fall enough upon their arse
in Africa.

II

(During Mr. Botha's visit to the whitish states of Europe,
his wife Elize, the honorable, misplaced a diamond and
gold ring worth $80,000. Two charwomen working at
Heathrow Airport found the ring while cleaning the South
African Airways plane which had borne both Bothas to
London. As their reward they each received thirty pounds,
@ $65, and lunch on a South African Airways jet—going
nowhere.)

The tiny item in the *New York Times*
failed to mention either woman's name
But thirty pounds is a lot for unnamed women
who have to bring up families of children
often alone.

Dressed in their best for lunch, they board the plane
parked on the tarmac, greet the hostess by her name.

She's told of theirs; asks them to be seated
So terribly sorry—could their names be once repeated?
Politeness reigns, and now they will be treated
to a meal of gammon, fried potatoes, wine
from South Africa. "Don't you think it fine?"
Not wanting a response, she ladles out their grub.
"Thank you, madam, I prefer the Courage at my pub,"
one guest responds, looks to her friend and smiles,
"Thirty bloody quid," she thinks, "that woman must have
        piles."

The newfound ring, elaborately tasteful band,
has been restored to its deeply suntanned hand
The lady stretches back, regards her decoration
"Was it given, madam, for some particular occasion?"
"Yes, indeed, the anniversary of our nation's separation.
I had no idea it would be returned, if found.
I thought by now it would be underground,
on the Black market, melted into bits
The very thought could send me into fits
of despair; I'm sure you know
how any sort of loss can lay you low.
The stones are from my country, the gold as well,
mined from a pit half-again as deep as hell.
Our mines go very far into the earth,
these things are rare; I can't say what they're worth."

The woman who drinks bitter takes this in
The hostess tries her patience, she gives in
to feelings triggered by the lady's words
she needs to speak, yet hopes she won't be heard.
"I know summat about the mines; my brother is on strike
in Sheffield. If you care, I can tell you what it's like
to work for days on end in long stone halls
with eardrums bursting when the hammer falls
your life, it seems, is drawn on dripping walls."

"He's white, of course. Our Zulus are the ones
who travel down to find the diamonds,
like crippled Vulcans—gods of mines and fire—
my goodness, how those people can perspire!"

(Why are white people so concerned with race,
determined to hold the darker ones in place?
Is it really just because of someone's color
or money, too, the usual cause of bother?)

"My brother mines to make a decent wage
I've heard you pay your miners with a page
of debts, and hope their labor dulls their rage.
My brother mines, but he's treated like a man
and if he's not, he can do what he can
like calling strike with all his working mates.
You might consider that, before the time is late."

"Whatever do you mean? What cheek! I never!
I suppose your friend believes she's something clever."
Addressing the other guest, she expects some reassurance
She's been tested far beyond a hostess' endurance
Fancy a woman who cleans toilets for a living
Advising her on the treatment Pretoria ought be giving
their Zulus!

"Pardon me, madam," the other woman speaks,
"But my friend has had no decent rest for weeks
Her littlest one has had a dreadful flu
But she must char, so what is one to do?
Can't hire minders, madam, just not paid enough
So having a sick child is bloody rough
Excuse me, madam, didn't mean to curse,
but I expect your kiddies had a nurse."

(No need to speak for me or make amends
Don't tell her things she just can't understand.)

"Forgive if I spoke, madam, out of turn
But I have anger that would make you burn."

(I didn't want to smile, apologize
but losing thirty quid would not be wise.
Our council flat is dingy, far too small
We need some colored paper on the wall.)

"Thanks for lunch, madam, I'm sure I'm delighted
Please excuse, if by my words I slighted
your lovely country; you know best, I'm sure
exactly what your people can endure."

7811 St. Peter/Schwarzwald (700–1200 m)
Seminar- und Pfarrkirche
Erbaut von Peter Thumb (1724–1727)

May 25, 1991.

Dear Jeannine – nochmals nachträglich
meine allerbesten Wünsche zu
Deinem Geburtstage! Das beiliegende
Bild ist zwar nicht das, das ich für Dich
erwerben will – jedoch möge ich, dass es
Dir gefallen wird. Ich hoffe es wird –
geklappt und findet es sehr schön und
apropos für Dich —

Ja, wünsche Dir einen schönen,
erholsamen Sommer.

Deine

Schwarzwald-Verlag GmbH, Postfach 2220, 7601 Offenburg · Ges. gesch. Nr. 594

I-tie-all-my-people-together

Mo so awọn enia mi po

Oshun makes of her people one
Mo so awọn enia mi po

healer   destroyer of cruelty
mother   bringer of judgment
lover   excelling in tenderness
guardian   punishing foolishness

she lives at the bottom of the river
she greets the most important matter in the water

generous fury
calm intelligence
burning sweetness

she smites the belly of the liar with her bell

mistress of àshe, *of full predictive power*

she is coolness.

There is an old man standing behind me in a darkened hall.
He might be standing in the high grass of a treeless savannah.

I shut the door and turn around.

Àshe is a concept central to Yoruban belief. It is defined by Thompson as "the power to make things happen." It is the gift of Olorun, God Almighty.

There is an old man watching me in this darkened hall.
He might be watching his cattle graze near the River Niger.

The old man and I face each other   stand exactly eye-to-eye.
He might be facing a woman come back from bartering
        firewood.

Whitened hair circles the brownness of his skull
Whitened beard fringes his soft round chin.

He is not a dream. Is he a messenger?
I do not know him. How could I have created him?
His eyes are large. He is silent as he regards me.

The old man stands   his cape over one shoulder
is made of strip-woven cloth.
He might be squatting in a marketplace in Abomey.
What has he come to tell me?

The cape he wears has colors—brown and black
        predominate—
but this is a darkened hall and all other colors are lost in its
shadows.

The old man carries a walking staff, a spear.
He might be traveling across a ridge near the Black Volta
seeking a friend.

Long, dark wood is tipped with an iron blade—dull-colored,
        oval.
The blade reaches past his right shoulder. He leans against his
staff as he regards me.

He is complete. How could he belong here?
What has brought him?

They are calling his name in some village right now.
Wondering where he has disappeared to. What would anyone
want with this old man?

There might be guns aimed at his head in Sharpeville.

I need him
The fingers of his right hand wrap around his staff.
He has come a long way to find me.

I feel an immense quiet around us.
There is not one sound. We have moved out of sound.
We are not in this house. Something holds us. We are not
in this time. We are caught somewhere. At this instant there is
nothing but us.

Stillness.
I can see by his eyes that he knows me.
That he has come all this way to tell me.

The street sounds   he is gone.

Italicized passages are taken from a Yoruban hymn to Oshun, found
in Robert Farris Thompson, *Flash of the Spirit* (Random House,
1984).

Other titles from Firebrand Books include:

Jonestown & Other Madness, Poetry by Pat Parker

Mohawk Trail by Beth Brant (*Degonwadonti*)

Moll Cutpurse, A Novel by Ellen Galford

My Mama's Dead Squirrel, Lesbian Essays on Southern Culture by Mab Segrest

The Sun Is Not Merciful, Short Stories by Anna Lee Walters